MANAGING
IT
AS A BUSINESS

A Survival Guide
for CEOs

Mark D. Lutchen

WILEY

John Wiley & Sons, Inc.

Published by John Wiley & Sons, Inc., Hoboken, New Jersey.
Published simultaneously in Canada.

For general information on our other products and services, or technical support, please contact our Customer Care Department within the United States at 800-762-2974, outside the United States at 317-572-3993 or fax 317-572-4002.

Wiley also publishes its books in a variety of electronic formats. Some content that appears in print may not be available in electronic books. For more information about Wiley products, visit our web site at www.wiley.com.

Library of Congress Cataloging-in-Publication Data:

Lutchen, Mark D.
  Managing IT as a business : a survival guide for CEOs / Mark D. Lutchen.
     p. cm.
Includes index.
  ISBN 0-471-47104-6 (cloth)
  1. Information technology—Management.   2. Information resources management. I. Title.
  HD30.2.L88   2004
  004′.068—dc22

                                                          2003017893

Printed in the United States of America.

10 9 8 7 6 5

To my family—
You light up my life!

Contents

Foreword

On May 22, 2003, CIOs from many of the world's largest companies convened for the annual MIT CIO Summit. As each CIO spoke, a common theme quickly emerged: CIOs were under unprecedented pressure to deliver measurable productivity benefits. The free-spending days of the late 1990s were over.

There is no question that the current focus on productivity is an essential return to reality. In the past, hundreds of billions of IT dollars have been wasted either because no metrics were used, or, worse, because the wrong metrics were used. Unfortunately, IT productivity has too often been defined by an overly simplistic question: "How can we squeeze the IT budget even further?"

Stephen Norman of Merrill Lynch was one of the CIOs at the Summit. He captured this mind-set evocatively when he told the story of the "Magic Orange":

> On a clear December day, a worried-looking CFO knocked on the door of his harried CIO and said, "Times are tough. We need to squeeze 10% out of the IT budget." With some effort and with more than a little help from Moore's law, the CIO managed to squeeze out 10% of costs without causing any appreciable loss in service quality. The following year his CFO returned to say, "That was terrific. However, this year we need to squeeze out *another* 10%." Dutifully, with some hard-nosed decision making, the CIO managed to find an additional 10%. However, at the end of the year, the CFO once again said, "Now we need an additional 10%. And, what's more, you can guess what I'll be asking for next year." The CIO took a deep breath. It was getting really difficult to squeeze out

more savings. He wondered how often he could wring the same orange and still get drinkable juice. To the CFO, the IT department was a "Magic Orange" that could be squeezed indefinitely.

While achieving cost savings in the IT department is a laudable goal, doing so risks missing the bigger picture. The real productivity benefits from the remarkable increase in computing power per dollar do not come merely from cost savings in the IT budget.

Rather, as Mark Lutchen clearly illustrates in this book, those savings result from thinking of IT more broadly as a business. That means delivering more value to the rest of the organization by increasing the productivity of other business units, of end-users, and of the corporation as a whole.

Indeed, research now clearly shows that on average, firms that are more IT intensive also are more productive over time.* More interesting, however, are findings that indicate a tremendous disparity in returns. Some very high IT spenders excel while others perform poorly. As an investment, IT may have a positive expected return, but that return is not guaranteed.

What differentiates successful investors from their competitors? As Lutchen argues in this book, to be effective, IT must link to corporate strategy. The IT organization should be aligned with the underlying profitability drivers of the business. At the same time, business systems must be redesigned to take advantage of new, low cost, and more powerful technologies as they become available. To achieve these objectives, CIOs must build strong and trusting relationships with their peers on the executive management team, with business-unit CEOs, and with the key end-users, that is, customers. Also, they must be ready, willing, and able to transform their businesses and workflows so that these truly leverage the technology. Indeed, a whole new digital organization is needed if businesses are to benefit fully from IT.

In my own research, I've found that for every dollar spent on IT hardware, up to nine dollars go to complementary investments, including organizational and human capital. These investments can create real, if intangible, assets. A CIO who focuses only on IT spending that occurs within the IT

---

* In a study of over 500 large U.S. firms, Lorin Hitt and I found that IT intensity correlates with both productivity levels and productivity growth. Erik Brynjolfsson and Lorin Hitt, "Computing Productivity: Firm-level Evidence," *Review of Economics and Statistics* (2003), available from http://ebusiness.mit.edu/erik.

budget misses all but the tip of the iceberg. This can have disastrous results. While many of these intangible assets go unmeasured on typical corporate balance sheets, they should not go unmanaged. Taken as a whole, Lutchen's ideas for understanding the "real" level of IT spending provide a welcome and useful framework for addressing this challenge and opportunity.

This book will prove invaluable to CEOs, CIOs, CTOs, CFOs, business-unit leaders, consultants, and researchers who seek a practical, research-grounded guide to running IT as a business. There was a time when IT in many firms could be relegated to a cost center, but, today, every industry is a high-tech industry. As a result, no successful manager can afford to ignore the lessons that Lutchen provides.

The author's advice is grounded in a unique combination of careful research and real-world experience that Mark Lutchen brings to all of his work. As one of the Founding Sponsors of the MIT Center for eBusiness, PricewaterhouseCoopers, as represented by Lutchen and his colleagues, consistently challenged us to push the frontiers of research in directions that would create tangible benefits for businesses. That ethos infuses this book and makes it an "essential read" for anyone hoping to achieve such benefits.

The power of IT has been growing exponentially for more than 40 years. Today's computers literally have 10 million times more processing power than the computers used in the 1960s. This trend is sure to continue for at least another decade. In fact, all signs indicate that it is accelerating. More importantly, the domain of activities affected by IT is vastly larger than it was 40 or even 10 years ago. In short, the impact of IT that we've seen during the past decade is only a fraction of what we can expect to see during the decade to come.

The implication is clear. CEOs and CIOs who don't learn to manage IT as a business will lose their mandate. Those who do will be the business leaders of the next decade. That is why I urge all who aspire to such leadership to read and profit from this book.

ERIK BRYNJOLFSSON
George Schussel Professor of Management
and Information Technology
Director, MIT Center for eBusiness
MIT Sloan School of Management
Cambridge, Massachusetts

Acknowledgments

Authoring a book such as this is analogous to conducting a world-class symphony orchestra. Like the conductor, the author moves to center stage at the end of the performance and takes the bow for the result of the collective work of many individuals. That is how I feel about writing this book. Were it not for the behind-the-scenes work of many people who are unable to take the bow with me, I would not be in a position to do so. I am truly humbled by the amount of talent, intellect, creativity, integrity, and professionalism exhibited during the writing of this book by my clients, partners, colleagues, and other professional associates who toiled alongside me both in substance and in spirit. Thanking specific people is always a risky business because someone is always inadvertently left out. I apologize up front if that occurs here; it is surely not my intent.

First, I would like to gratefully acknowledge a few people whose influence and assistance were invaluable. In a professional services firm, clients always come first, so my initial thanks go to all of the clients who have afforded me the opportunity to be of service to them during the past three decades. Helping many of the world's top companies to solve some very complex problems has provided me with a wealth of unparalleled experience, some of which I have tried to share in this book. I would particularly like to thank Donard Gaynor, former CFO, SVP-HR, CIO, and reengineering leader of The Seagram Spirits and Wine Group; Nick Henny, vice chairman and CFO of Universal Music Group; and Paul Turner, executive VP and CTO of AMS for applying their unique business insights to their reviews of this manuscript.

Next, I would like to thank a number of people who were instrumental in researching, writing, editing, and publishing this book. These include

Gene Zasadinski, my editor at PricewaterhouseCoopers; Mark Friedlich, PwC's global publisher; and Jon Zonderman, freelance editorial consultant. Gene, Mark, and Jon—your professionalism and steady hands kept this effort on course and on schedule with the highest quality. You are truly all masters at your respective crafts. A special thanks also goes to Denis Picard, a partner of mine who began this literary adventure with me, but who is now breaking new ground in applying the principles discussed here, as well as a few of his own, as a businessman, advisor, and CIO. I would also like to acknowledge the outstanding work of all the people at John Wiley & Sons, especially editor Airie Stuart, publisher Larry Alexander, and associate marketing director Laurie Harting. Thanks for believing in the value of the message contained in this book and for ever so carefully shepherding the manuscript through the publishing process.

While this book was being written, I was also in the process of building and leading an IT Business Risk Management practice for Pricewaterhouse-Coopers. The core team of people involved in that effort deserves a big thank you for helping me to codify and simplify much of what is discussed in this text into a service that can be provided to our clients on a much broader and consistent basis than ever before. Thank you, Jonathan Lawrence, Sam Tobin, Dries Bredenkamp, Anu Sahi, and Ellen Fang. And thank you, Paul Kennedy, for your constructive insights and input along the way.

During the past several years, I have been a member of the executive board of the MIT/Sloan Center for eBusiness, which is very ably led by its chairman, Dean Emeritus Glen Urban, and its director, Schussel Professor of Management Erik Brynjolfsson. I have developed the highest respect and admiration for both of these gentlemen as I have watched them build one of MIT/Sloan School's flagships of intellectual pursuit and practical business application.

My thanks must also go to individuals with whom I worked when I had the pleasure of co-leading PricewaterhouseCoopers' Multinational Corporation (MNC) Network. If it were not for my partners, including Pat Kiernan, Dick Rossi, Bill Glimour, Bob Leach, George Barbee, Howard Aycock, and Paul Turner, who is currently executive vice president and CTO of AMS, and for outside expert advisors such as Ken Roman, former chairman and CEO of Ogilvy & Mather Worldwide, the client service and teaming principles created, established, and followed within the Network would not have flourished and become cornerstones of this book.

It is often easy to overlook the outstanding executive and administrative support and assistance that hard-working individuals provide selflessly and without fail day in and day out. Thank you to my executive assistant, Catherine Zadroga, who, for the past 21 years, has, with professionalism and good humor, faithfully kept things on track and in order.

I would also like to thank a few groups of special people who worked long and hard to prove to many skeptics that the principles espoused in this book really do deliver results. To people on the TSSLT: Even though I cannot name everyone, each of you knows who you are and what your contributions were to the team, and for that I cannot thank you enough. Thank you to Larry Phelan, Joe DeTullio, and Rich Poshpeck—you know all too well what it really took to turn the ship with speed and passion. I would also like to thank Kathy Leach and Mary Linda Denton for making communicating so easy; Brian Moxey for always making the logistics work out; Stacey Foster and Roberta Perry for taking HR to new levels; Bob Brick and Jim Holloway for your strategic and technology insights; Jennifer Eckler, Pat Straughn, Nancy Browning, Cindy Cole, Bud Murphy, Sheryl Mills, Dave Goodman, Daryl Mattson, Marty Porea, Lee Robinson, and a host of others for always rising to the challenge; Robert Kight and Mike Drosdowski for establishing a security organization that is second to none; Bob Buttacavoli, Mark McGovern, Roy Ogura, Mike Williams, Sean D'Souza, Shawn Connors, and the rest of the Genesis team for creating a platform that continues to thrive; and Bill Yant, for your insightful and steady guidance. Thanks also to Gregg Ward of Orlando-Ward & Associates for your unique communications creativity and to all of my international colleagues around the world who clearly demonstrated how diversity and multinational capabilities always make a team better and stronger.

Finally, to the hundreds of outstanding people who comprised Team TSS around the world, you are truly the ones who made it all happen on the ground. You learned to embrace change; you successfully addressed some of the most complex, global IT management and technical problems; and you created an unparalleled world-class, high-performance, and top-quality team. To each of you—and you know who you are—I respectfully tip my hat and want you all to know, once again, how inspirational and rewarding it was to work with you.

MARK D. LUTCHEN

Introduction

To: The Executive Leadership Team
        The Board of Directors

From: The New CIO

For years now, our company's information technology (IT) organization has mirrored the way the company itself has evolved—decentralized, fragmented, and underleveraged. While significant sums of money have been spent, lack of focus and vision has lessened the potential impact of those expenditures. Specifically:

- IT has never had a global vision or strategy.
- IT expenditures have not been effectively leveraged across the company.
- IT has been managed as a cost center rather than as a strategic competitive enabler and revenue enhancer.
- IT has not been an integral part of our business planning and execution; at best, IT has been a less than effectively managed afterthought.
- IT leadership has been fragmented and diffused within the company, severely limiting the IT organization's ability to drive and leverage standards to benefit the business.
- IT has not had a single focal point responsible and accountable for leading, managing, and leveraging our investment.
- Our IT "spend" across the company is second only to that for human resources and is one of the largest investments and expenditures in our budget. This sizable strategic investment has not been effectively managed.

While we have made considerable strides during the past few years in addressing some of these issues, we still have significant work to complete if we are to accomplish our overall mission.

With our business becoming increasingly complex, it is essential that we evolve and enhance the current technology planning process to reflect the changes that have occurred in our businesses. In that regard, we must develop a new, fully linked technology planning process that is more product-line focused than our current approach.

We need to work together to develop a framework that will enable us to accomplish these objectives. It is only when I work closely with the entire executive leadership team and the board and have a legitimate "seat at the table" that we can meet these goals.

Thank you for your kind attention to this urgent matter.

This memo, which was actually written by a newly appointed chief information officer (CIO), could have been composed by hundreds of other former or current CIOs. The notion that executive leaders are not as involved or familiar with IT as they should be is not new. In his 1991 book, *Managing IT at the Board Level: The Hidden Agenda Exposed,* Kit Grindley wrote the following paragraphs.

"Once it was all about trade, the days of the great merchants. Then it was about production, and the engineer was king. When the critical path became raising and deploying capital, the accountant held sway. Recently, consumerism has brought the marketer to power. In the future, it's clear that power and success will accompany the management of information resources."[1]

He continues, "[But] those who run the businesses have enormous difficulty accepting that IT is a part of the business strategy. For centuries, business has been about making things, marketing things, and managing money. Businessmen have done their job and earned their living by being expert in one or more of these areas."[2]

---

[1] Kit Grindley, *Managing IT at the Board Level: The Hidden Agenda Exposed,* London: Pittman Publishing (1991), p. 23.
[2] Ibid., p. 50.

THE EVOLUTION OF IT

Information technology (IT) is one of the top three-to-five expenditures in most large corporations. In the late 1990s, it was not unusual for each of the 500 largest global companies to spend $200 million, $500 million, even $1 billion annually on IT addressing Y2K computer issues and the conversion of European national currencies to the euro, ramping up an e-business presence, implementing enormous global enterprise resource planning (ERP) systems, or just keeping day-to-day IT operations running.

Beginning in 2000, much of that IT spending fell off, once again putting many of these same companies behind the information technology curve. As capital spending by companies contracted, a disproportionate amount of that contraction affected spending on new IT.

Historically, IT has also been one of the least understood expenditures and one of the most mismanaged areas of many businesses. Inability to meld IT organizations, systems, and technology and to directly link these to the company's strategic business drivers to produce results is one of the major reasons why large, complex mergers or acquisitions often fail to deliver on their promised synergies.

If technology is to fulfill its promise and provide maximum benefit to a corporation, two major changes must occur:

1. The IT organization must be managed and led in a professional manner, like any large business unit, with careful attention to priorities, people, and performance.
2. The relationship between IT users throughout the corporation and the IT organization must change. IT users must understand that a company's ability to provide IT is not unlimited. Like anything else, IT is bound by rules of supply, demand, and cost. Only when users of IT throughout the corporation are forced to "pay" for IT, either explicitly through some sort of transfer pricing or more often implicitly through tradeoffs in other corporate budget line items, will they learn how to use IT carefully and purposefully.

Neither change, however, is easily accomplished. Individuals who lead IT organizations have generally come up from the technology side of the equation and have not traditionally possessed the well-developed, finely honed business management, leadership, organizational, political, and communication skills necessary to lead complex organizations effectively. Many technology leaders also lack the ability to provide direct, substantive, and easy-to-understand help to top corporate executives who must leverage IT if they are to drive the enterprise to new heights.

At most companies, IT leaders (CIOs) lack the support they need to acquire the necessary skills to participate at the top level of corporate management. In fact, at many companies, the CIO reports through the chief financial officer (CFO) or chief operating officer (COO). This often sends a message to the corporate leadership team, business-unit leaders, and the IT organization itself: Information technology (and information systems) is a *support function* and a *cost center* akin to accounting or facilities management rather than the important driver of business success that IT can and should be.

Such a message breeds constant tension between CIOs desiring more "toys" and CFOs looking on IT organizations as being expensive and, therefore, ripe for cutting and subjects the IT organization to endless, frustrating cycles of stop-and-start investment. It also inserts a layer between the CEO and a key person who has, or should have, a deep understanding of how the business really works and of the obstacles keeping the business from improving.

Because of this dichotomy between the *techies* and the *ties,* corporate IT spending is often haphazard, IT strategy is often not linked closely with business strategy, and IT projects often become captive to the business cycle when, in order to capture the advantages of new technologies, they should be continuous.

Another obstacle to maximizing the benefits of IT is the belief that IT is virtually impossible to measure and that only hard-core technical operations and discreet projects lend themselves to any sort of quantitative performance measurement. This belief has prevented broad-based, business-focused performance measurement concepts, processes, tools, and techniques from entering the IT organization. In reality, while embedding business-oriented performance measurements into all of the components of an IT organization (i.e., technical, functional, operational, and human) may not be easy, doing so is a necessity, a business imperative whose time has come. More and more executives tell me that this must be done if the IT organization is to survive in the twenty-first century.

The real conundrum here is that if this narrow view of IT is not sufficiently broadened, if the management of IT is not professionalized, and if users do not learn how to "price" IT against other corporate needs appropriately, companies will lose the opportunity to take advantage of proven and emerging technologies that can enhance their business's portfolios and revenues. The risk is that some existing players and new market entrants *will* take and apply a broader view of IT, placing those companies that do not at a competitive disadvantage.

VIEWING IT AS A BUSINESS UNIT

Historically, companies have attempted to address these issues by focusing either on the top or on the bottom of what might be termed the *IT Delivery Spectrum* (Figure I.1), that is, focusing either on strategy or on implementation of systems and infrastructure.

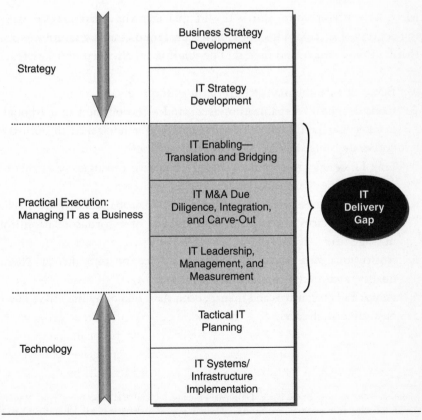

Figure I.1   IT Delivery Spectrum.

The main reason IT organizations and CIOs fail to deliver value to the business is their inability to focus sufficient attention and resources on the area in the middle—the *IT Delivery Gap*. While a significant portion of an organization's IT budget is spent on the complex fusion of technology processes and human assets that comprise IT infrastructure and IT management,[3] not enough management attention or management skill is focused there. For the most part, IT managers have traditionally not been schooled in weighing IT business risks against costs. Failure to address these areas affects the key IT business value levers, resulting in increased costs, higher business risks, and a reduced ability to manage and leverage the investment portfolio, thus limiting the overall business value of IT. Many of the problems on which I have been asked to advise have their roots in the company's failure to manage the key IT business value levers.

A New Solution

Many have attempted to address this IT management dilemma with varying degrees of success. This book, however, proposes a new solution—one that is at once simple and radical. The solution involves six critical steps:

1. Bring IT into the mainstream of the enterprise.
2. Consider the IT organization as a stand-alone business unit (though not necessarily a profit center) that advances the agenda of both the corporate center and the various business units.
3. Link IT strategy to corporate strategy, but with a focus on practical execution rather than theory and idealized processes.
4. Require business units to define their IT needs and require IT to provide services through a methodology of rigorous relationship management.
5. Institutionalize a culture of customer service, on-time delivery, high quality, and results-oriented performance.
6. Reward IT executives and managers on their outcomes that drive business value at all levels.

---

[3] For a detailed discussion, see Peter Weill, Mani Subramani, and Marianne Broadbent, "Building IT Infrastructure for Strategic Agility," *Sloan Management Review* (Fall, 2002): 57–65.

IT, like any other business unit, should not be about projects and processes, but about relationships, execution to plan, measurable outcomes, and people/skills development.

To evolve the IT organization to such a model, CEOs and CIOs must jointly enlist the support of other corporate executives, board members, and—where appropriate—financial buyers (venture capitalists and private equity investors) to drive the process.

CIOs must be brought to the executive management table, and once there, be expected to think and function as other executives do. If the current CIO's management skills are deficient, he or she must be helped to upgrade those skills or a new CIO needs to be found (not that it is easy currently to find one with stellar management, relationship development, people, and communication skills).

The corporate executive team must work with the CIO to assemble a top-notch management team. An IT leadership team in a large organization must have the equivalent of a business-unit COO and CFO, as well as dedicated human resources staff to help recruit, train, and retain the best quality employees and to remove, when necessary, those who do not measure up to current standards.

CIOs need to be supported by marketing and communications professionals who can help them communicate more effectively with technology users throughout the organization and make the black box of technology more transparent to IT constituencies, from the shop floor to the executive suite.

CEOs and CIOs must work with CFOs and COOs to craft relevant and executable IT strategy; create strategically focused yet tactically deliverable (*stractical*) plans; negotiate goals, objectives, resources, and budgets; and develop meaningful, laser-focused IT metrics by which to measure the success of the IT business. CEOs, CFOs, and COOs must talk about IT throughout the enterprise and must become knowledgeable users of IT services themselves if they are truly to understand the relationship between IT providers and users. In short, IT must operate like a business.

If IT people are ever to master the ability to cope effectively with a constant and continuous stream of rapid business and technology change, CIOs must lead by example. To accomplish all of this, they must instill a new culture throughout the IT organization—a culture based on customer focus, high quality, peak performance, and agility and flexibility. During three decades of advising companies concerning IT management, I have met only a few individuals who have really set out to master this model.

Future generations of CIOs must be rotated through operating units and other corporate functions to become more well-rounded business leaders. Their career paths must include hands-on education in management, finance, organizational skills, marketing, and communications, as well as in technology training.

Companies would not dare appoint a business-unit CEO who did not successfully apprentice throughout multiple organizations within the company, both functionally and geographically, to ensure that the candidate was well rounded. Succession planning is critical for top positions. Why then, do companies not have the same expectations for CIOs?

To manage IT as a business, a CEO and his or her executive leadership team must have a conceptual understanding of how technology can support business growth. Unless technology is implemented with the understanding that it may change how a company works, it will not reap the expected benefits. This book provides executive leaders, board members, and economic buyers with that conceptual understanding, as well as with an understanding of what their roles are in interacting with the CIO, the IT team, and the technology that is implemented.

A TECHNOLOGY VALUE OPTIMIZATION LENS

Finally, for the CIO and other business leaders to "speak the same language," a business-focused nomenclature, or uniform "lens," needs to be created for IT.

The IT management lens is just such a tool. As illustrated in Figure I.2, the framework consists of six critical drivers of IT success. Within each driver are from one to four component levers (a total of 14) that must be managed.

Alignment

This performance driver includes three component levers that deal with the ability to identify, highlight, plan for, measure, and improve on the critical areas that drive a quality IT organization and directly links these to the business's strategies and objectives. These component levers are important in ensuring that the focus of IT is always the same as the focus of the business.

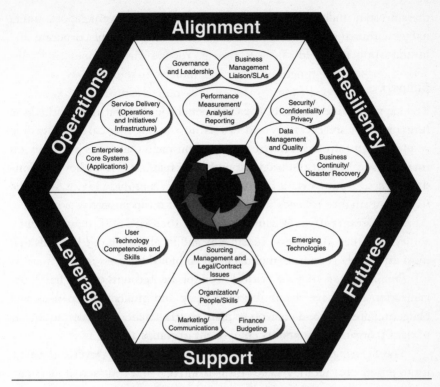

Figure I.2   IT Management Lens.

IT Governance and Leadership involves (1) the ability to focus, lead, and govern the activities and efforts of centralized and locally dispersed IT staff to enable them to deliver cost-effective, world-class IT services in a high-performance manner; (2) the ability to build a culture of continuous improvement of IT management processes, controls, and support based on internal and external best practices; and (3) the ability to establish a vision and strategy directly linked to key business objectives.

The *Business Management Liaison* has the ability to work effectively with multiple stakeholders and to apply customer relationship management practices, including the identification of appropriate, mutually agreed objectives, levels of service, and costs/service fees, which in turn are defined in service level agreements (SLAs).

Performance Measurement/Analysis Reporting is accomplished through the ability to effectively measure and analyze various aspects of performance of the IT organization and its service delivery capability and to present clear, understandable, and transparent performance reports internally (within the IT organization) and externally (to key corporate and business-unit stakeholders).

Support

The support driver includes four component levers that deal with those functions that are necessary and critical to the ongoing care and feeding (support) of a fully operational business entity and that focus primarily on financial and human resource management issues, as well as key relationships. These are important in ensuring that IT is provided with all of the requisite assistance it needs to operate as a full business entity.

The *Organization/People/Skills* lever focuses on IT management's ability to harness the diverse centralized and locally deployed IT skills that most effectively support complex global and local business needs.

Finance/Budgeting is a critical need for any business unit. The IT organization must have the ability to develop and implement financial and budgeting processes and controls to manage effectively the economic aspects of the IT organization and its component operations.

The *Sourcing Management and Legal/Contract Issues* lever is the ability to ensure that all IT-related third-party legal and contractual issues are handled in an appropriate manner.

Marketing/Communications is the ability to establish and maintain a variety of effective and efficient channels of open communication, dialogue, and discussion across all business units and geographies, as well as within the IT organization.

Operations

The operations driver is made up of two levers that deal with the fundamental inner workings of an IT organization—24/7 infrastructure service delivery and the development and maintenance of core application systems. These are important because they constitute the primary "manufacturing plant" of an IT organization.

Service Delivery (Operations and Initiatives/Infrastructure) is the ability to provide in a cost-effective manner user-oriented continuous services that are driven by business-oriented performance metrics.

The *Enterprise Core Systems* (Applications) lever enables the cost-effective implementation, maintenance, and rationalization of common and business-unit specific applications based on business-issue priorities.

Resiliency

The resiliency driver is made up of two levers that deal with the overall protection of enterprisewide IT assets—hardware, software, networks, services, and people—to prevent situations from occurring that could potentially cause major damage and disruption not only to the IT infrastructure, but also to the entire company. These are important in ensuring that the IT organization has the ability and agility to proactively adapt to constant change and negative conditions.

Security/Confidentiality/Privacy is the ability to work closely and effectively with the corporate risk management/security organization to ensure that the company's technology assets and networks are used and operated in the most secure and confidential manner possible, and in accordance with desired privacy constraints.

Data Management and Quality is the ability to ensure the completeness, accuracy, and integrity of critical data and the adequacy of the internal control environment to sustain the quality of the data over time. Also included are the collection, normalization, and analysis of large volumes of critical data in a controlled environment.

Business Continuity/Disaster Recovery is the ability to keep the IT organization and operations functioning in the event of various forms of business interruptions.

Leverage

The leverage driver has one lever, *User Technology Competencies and Skills,* which is the ability to encourage, support, and facilitate the continuous building and enhancement of IT literacy across the entire organization, enabling users to derive maximum benefit from IT assets.

Futures

The futures driver has one lever, *Emerging Technologies,* which is having the ability and vision to always be cognizant of the leading of technology with regard to any appropriate applications of such technology within the company.

Table I.1 compares a company that manages IT as a back-office support function/cost center to a company that manages IT as a business with respect to ways each look at these 14 items.

To gauge the size of the IT management gap, it is necessary to examine all 14 technology value optimization levers against their current state

Table I.1 Broadening the Executive Lens on IT

Competency Area	Managing IT as a Back-Office Support Function/Cost	Managing IT as a Business
Alignment		
Governance and leadership.	IT centric.	IT-business teaming.
Business management liaisons/SLAs.	IT-only ownership.	Joint IT-business accountability.
Performance measurement/analysis/reporting.	Primarily operational metrics.	Business value metrics.
Support		
Organization/people/skills.	Bureaucratic/hierarchical.	Adaptive, flexible, agile.
Finance/budgeting.	Cost containment.	Activity-based, investment portfolio.
Sourcing management and legal/contract issues.	Vendors as suppliers.	Partnering with vendors.
Marketing/communications.	Task related.	Open, candid, relationship oriented.
Operations		
Service delivery (operations and initiatives/infrastructure).	Infrastructure as reactive afterthought.	Strategic architecture as a competitive advantage.
Enterprise core systems (applications).	Individual applications—project driven.	Integrated application systems strategy.
Resiliency		
Security/confidentiality/privacy.	Defensive.	Strategic and offensive.
Business continuity/disaster recovery.	Reactive.	Planned and continuously updated.
Data management and quality.	Problem/reconciliation focused, reactive.	Engineered, structured, proactive.
Leverage		
User technology competencies and skills.	User determined.	Standardized and certified.
Futures		
Emerging technologies.	Follower.	Innovative.

and a future desired state that would enable business success. This future state is defined across four elements:

1. **P**olicy/risk
2. **O**rganization/people
3. **P**rocess/procedures/controls
4. **S**ystems/technology.

Easily understood by executives, these four categories, *POPS* for short, typically provide specific logical channels of responsibility and accountability for executing, managing, and monitoring improvement action plans.

Too often, IT leaders and managers fail to deliver value to the business because they oversimplify and focus only on a single point within the IT management and delivery framework. Instead, they must concentrate the need to fully integrate and link strategies, plans, actions, results, and measurement across the six management value drivers. This inability to "connect the dots" across all of the various drivers creates serious business risk within today's increasingly complex IT environments.

The bottom line is straightforward. IT is a complex wild animal that can be tamed only when it is managed in the same way as any other successful business. CEOs, board members, other executives, and financial buyers must learn to be "animal trainers." Today, many do not know what to do when they get in the cage—in fact, many deliberately stay out of the cage because of what they do not know about technology.

But if they are to harness IT's power to create value for the enterprise, they need to get into the cage. And to get into the cage with confidence, they need to know that like any other animal in the corporate circus, IT can be tamed by running it in a businesslike way and by building the business case that IT can, if managed in this way, move the company closer to its goals and objectives.

That has been my experience as an executive, a CIO, and a business advisor, and that is what I am seeking to share with you in this book.

CHAPTER 1

Get the CIO on the Executive Team

The Chief Information Officer/Executive Reporting Relationship

At a major provider of information and other services, a new executive team had just arrived. The new chief executive officer (CEO) commissioned a complete review of all the company's corporate functions, with an eye toward modernizing and streamlining them to enable and support the customer-service teams in the field more effectively.

The review of the IT function was particularly disturbing to him because it revealed a huge weakness and gap in his ability to propel the company forward along the lines of his strategic plan. Without a chief information officer (CIO), IT was fragmented, unfocused, and uncontrolled.

The new CEO knew he had to appoint a CIO who understood the company's business issues, could build relationships with the key business-unit leaders, and could function as a member of the leadership team. Knowing the personalities of all the company's key executives, he also understood that the new CIO would have to earn his way onto the leadership team. The CEO also struggled with whether to have the new position report directly to himself or to the chief operating officer (COO). He decided he would ask the new CIO, an individual with many years of business experience, about his views concerning the reporting line.

During their discussion, the CEO suggested that he would like to have the CIO report to the COO, to whom the accounting and operations functions also reported. The new CIO raised a number of concerns. He was worried about the perception of this reporting relationship throughout the company and particularly among members of the executive leadership team. How, he wondered, would he get any respect or time from the leadership team if his role, while described as important, was still positioned beneath the leadership team level?

- He was also concerned about whether or not the COO, with whom he had never before worked, shared the CEO's views concerning the importance of IT and of the CIO's role. He would have to work quickly to create a relationship with the COO, and if the COO and the CEO were not on the same page, things could become difficult.
- Finally, he was truly concerned about not having easy access on a regular basis to the CEO and to members of the leadership team. He was afraid he was going to be insulated from the real business issues and would, therefore, not be very effective in executing his goals and responsibilities as CIO. He knew that because of his relationship with the CEO, he could probably gain access to him on short notice; but he was concerned that many members of the executive team would consider his doing that to be an "end run." He also felt that for him to be able to turn the CEO's vision for IT into reality, he needed easy access to the rest of the leadership team as well.

The new CIO proposed the following solution: He would officially report to the COO, but he also wanted to be a full-time, equal member of the leadership team and a full participant in all key business strategy and other meetings. This unique arrangement resonated with all parties.

By behaving like a businessman and working out this compromise, the CIO was able to get his "seat at the table" and reasonable access to the CEO and the rest of the executive team. The leadership team quickly came to view him as a management peer, not just a "techie" from IT, regardless of his official reporting relationship.

He quickly built a very good relationship with the COO, who gave him wide berth in terms of restructuring the IT organization. Because of the open, candid, and collegial working relationship between the COO and CIO, the COO was not concerned that the CIO had access to the CEO and did not fear that the CIO would use that access to go over his head. By focusing on creating ways to work together as business people, the CIO was able to carry out many of the changes that the CEO and senior leadership wanted to implement within the IT organization.

Strong market forces, globalization, and ever-increasing customer demands are causing the world's largest corporations to realize that technology plays an integral, mission-critical role in helping executives to meet key business objectives and, ultimately, to achieve their companies' visions. However, investing in technology that is not used to its fullest potential is wasteful and irresponsible and often indicates a fundamental breakdown in the basic management controls within the organization.

Such investing often occurs when a CIO is not considered to be an influential participant in strategic discussions and when the IT organization is not considered to be integral to the business strategy. The CIOs who are most effective at mapping technology to business goals are those who have the ear and the trust of business-unit leaders and the corporate leadership team. The IT organization needs to be inextricably tied to the business and, to provide true value, it must have the support of corporate and business-unit leadership, from the CEO and board of directors chairperson on down. This is not a simple issue of alignment or linkage; it is more akin to being "joined at the hip."

The CIO's role is becoming ever more complex. In the 1970s and 1980s, the CIO was, essentially, the head of corporate data processing. Today's CIO heads up a business unit that is responsible, in many cases, for maintaining technology infrastructure and communication networks; for upgrading, installing, and training users regarding ever-more-powerful business decision support application software; and for overseeing a program for annually leasing or purchasing hundreds or thousands of new pieces of computing or communication hardware and devices. The CIO's budget for people, maintenance, procurement, new projects, and consulting or outsourcing may run into the hundreds of millions of dollars.

In light of this changing role, what skills should the CIO possess? What are the CIO's primary responsibilities? Where does the CIO sit in relation to other organizational leaders? And finally, what must the CEO do to help develop and nurture the CIO?

- Ideally, company leadership should view the CIO as a valued member of the executive team who advises and demonstrates how technology could be used to achieve the corporation's vision and business objectives. But the CEO's job is to justify how implementing that technology can have a positive impact on realizing the company's vision.

- The CIO should have a front-row seat at all strategic business-planning sessions and advise on the role of technology. But the CIO should not make the final decisions about which technology investments make the most business sense.

- With the CEO, corporate business leaders, and business-unit leaders, the CIO decides which technology options map to the business vision and are good business investments. But the ultimate responsibility for making the business case rests with the various functional and business-unit leaders.

- Involvement of senior business management is critical to the development of an effective technology infrastructure. To achieve this kind of business advantage with technology, the CIO and business leaders must have a comfortable, open, and candid peer-to-peer working relationship, regardless of the reporting structure in place.

WHAT IS THE ROLE OF THE NEW CIO?

In 1999, the executive search firm Korn/Ferry International conducted a survey of 340 CIOs in the United States, United Kingdom, Germany, and France.* One of the key trends articulated in this study was that CIOs felt they were—or should be—on the verge of transitioning from a tactical role, where they are involved in the short-term technical planning and implementation of hardware and software, to a strategic role, where they are more involved in corporate planning.

The feeling of many of these CIOs (a feeling I sensed among many of my clients in the late 1990s) was that participation in technology planning for year 2000 (Y2K) systems issues, for the transition to a single European currency, and for the implementation of massive enterprise resource planning (ERP) systems represented the last hurrah of the tactical CIO.

---

* "The Changing Role of the Chief Information Officer," Korn/Ferry International (1998).

During the late 1990s, much new technology entered the marketplace. The "grocery shopping" method of acquisition—going down all of the aisles and buying one of every product category—hitherto embraced by CIOs became unfeasible. It became clear that CIOs were going to have to begin more rigorously to map technology opportunities to business drivers and corporate goals and that one technology solution could not fit all business profitability drivers.

A new role for the CIO quickly emerged, a role that would require the CIO to:

- Establish, implement, and communicate the strategic IT vision and plan, wedded to the overall business strategy
- Ensure that IT is used effectively to achieve overall business goals related to revenue growth, profitability, and cost effectiveness
- Build and continue to evolve relevant IT skills, capabilities, and teamwork across the enterprise
- Leverage technical expertise and minimize duplication of effort across the enterprise
- Coordinate and drive, where appropriate, IT policy, strategy, standards, common approaches, shared services, and sourcing arrangements throughout the corporation
- Serve as the point person (internally and externally), that is, as the company's *single voice for technology*.

As Michael Doane, vice president, Professional Services Strategies for META Group, Inc., puts it, "Over-acquisition of applications software from 1995–2001, combined with a slow economy, has led clients into an era of management and consolidation. CIOs are increasingly in search of measurable business value from what is spent on IT. Organizations across the board are not yet doing a very good job of balancing the needs of business and of IT."

Developing and Communicating the Strategic IT Vision and Plan

The strategic IT vision must be crisp, clear, and simple enough for every member of the company to understand without much explanation. It must be easy for executives, managers, IT people, and users throughout the company to remember it and repeat it. However, if it is to resonate with executive management, this vision must be firmly based on a good understanding of the company's underlying business strategies.

Size and volume do not matter with regard to the vision. A good clear vision can be presented on a single sheet of paper or presentation slide. The plan derived from this vision must have depth and substance and must be developed at the right level of detail so that it can be monitored effectively in terms of actions and measurable results.

Finally, both the vision and the plan must be communicated appropriately. The CIO must "walk the talk" with regard to IT, but so, too, must the CEO and other executives. Executives need to be able to articulate the vision to anyone who asks about it and must understand the plan just enough to know that they can trust the CIO to explain the plan in more detail to those who wish or need to know more.

If the CIO is the only person who can articulate the vision, he or she has not done a good job. Conversely, if the executive leaders understand the vision and do not articulate it, they are falling down on their job of providing the CIO with the necessary executive support needed to turn the vision into reality. In many companies that I have worked with, I have seen the creation of outstanding strategic IT visions and plans, but implementation and execution of these has fallen far short because of a failure to communicate them effectively and to achieve ownership across the organization.

Ensuring that IT Is Used Effectively

One of the biggest responsibilities of a corporate CIO is to keep the CEO from allowing inappropriate and sometimes wrong decisions to be made regarding IT spending. Buying technology just for the sake of acquiring the latest and greatest IT toys, or following the *fad du jour* (FDJ) is not a wise way to spend IT resources.

Often, much of this spending is driven by operating functions or business-unit leaders and their senior marketing or production staff or by semiknowledgeable IT "hobbyists," who hold themselves out as the business unit's technology aficionados. But the CIO must be able to stand up to such people and say, "I have the authority within this company to tell you that this is not an effective use of IT resources. If you feel strongly about this, you need to put it in your budget, and then I'll provide the necessary support for it. But I will not allow this to be dropped in my lap without my peers at the executive level signing off on it."

IT must be appropriate and adequate for the task at hand. Elephant guns should not be used to shoot flies or fly swatters to herd elephants. The right tools for the job may not be what everyone—or even what anyone—is using today or what anyone wants.

Therefore, IT needs must be clearly and carefully defined. Users do not always know what they need or even what they really want. The process of getting users to define their needs clearly is an evolving business analysis issue. IT people need to understand what business objectives users are trying to accomplish and then help them to understand what they are asking for and whether or not there are cost-effective solutions.

Most people date before they marry and test drive a car before they buy one. The same should apply to new IT. Both users and IT professionals should test new IT systems before they are turned on, going slowly and engaging in open communications about expectations and about the realities of the IT being implemented. A good and lasting "marriage" between IT and the business units evolves through a number of stages in a flexible and productive manner.

Building IT Skills and Capabilities

The skills needed in today's IT organization are as varied as those needed in any business unit in the company. All types of skills are necessary, not just technical skills. For IT people to advance, they need to develop capabilities related to project management, financial management, performance measurement, one-on-one and group communications as well as written communications, organizational and people development, and relationship management.

People and the skills they possess are the most important assets of an IT organization. Because of the rapid pace of change in technology, the technical and business analysis skills of each person working in the IT organization must be continually renewed and upgraded. It is also important that the IT organization foster the culture and spirit necessary for any high-performance team. Members must share experience and knowledge and help each other get the job done. As companies become more complex and networks beyond the company's four walls develop, IT teams must be like their counterpart business-unit teams in their ability to partner with other organizations in the network and to create fluid, virtual, performance-driven teams.

A technically competent leader who has no background in managing a business will not be able to help the IT organization develop these critical skills and cultural attributes. And a company that believes IT is merely a support function and should not be an integral part of the high-performance, cross-functional, and cross-corporate-boundary way of doing business will find itself left behind by competitors who are using IT to leverage business performance. I have worked with many excellent technology people whose lack of fundamental business management and organizational skills has astounded me. This dichotomy of skills clearly inhibited their ability to advance their well-intentioned IT agendas across their respective organizations.

Leveraging Global Technical Expertise

Although some part of IT, especially infrastructure, can be leveraged across business units and organizations around the world, other parts of the company's IT will, of necessity, be more local in focus, regardless of whether the company is organized by lines of business, product lines, countries, or regions. The watchword for IT should be "as global as necessary, as local as possible."

All IT best practices do not emanate from the United States. A CIO needs to understand the skills, capabilities, and accomplishments of the various IT teams and organizations throughout the world and to assign the best people, wherever they are located, to roles where they can help the rest of the IT organization to replicate their successes in their home regions.

Being a truly global IT organization is about deciding strategy and developing plans as one team and then allowing for local differences when determining how that strategy and those plans are executed. The local IT people understand both the IT imperatives and the local business culture. The CIO needs to listen to and respect local IT professionals and let them educate him or her as to the differences that need to be taken into consideration. Rather than trying to force things to be done in one way around the world, the CIO must leverage similarities and account for differences.

Managing IT as a global business is geometrically harder than managing IT as a business in a single, domestic environment. CEOs of global companies must try to fill the CIO slot with business people who have worked outside of the home country. Many of the CIOs that I have known who have mastered the issues of working globally have also gone on to become invaluable advisors to CEOs and other executives in their companies in terms of navigating the minefields of globalization.

Coordinating Policy, Strategy, Standards, and Approaches

The CIO resides at the *hub* of IT policy, strategy, standards, and approaches, rather than at the *pinnacle*. He or she must play the role of cheerleader and influencer, working with business units, the IT organization, executive leadership, and users in general to get them all on board.

The job can be lonely. Not everyone else in management will agree that CIOs need to be involved. Disputes about primacy and who drives processes will always occur, and some people will always believe that IT should be purely supportive of business and that the CIO should not have the authority to deny business units their IT requests.

A CIO must carefully pick his or her battles with regard to policy, strategy, standards, and approaches. The CIO needs to strive for ownership of these issues, both within the IT organization and the business in general. Once the CIO gets some level of agreement, his or her charter is to drive the implementation forward with discipline, rigor, and speed and to closely monitor performance against goals.

Being the *Single Voice for Technology*

The executive team wants and needs to be able to look to one person as the leader and focal point of any group, function, or organization within the company. This is as true for IT as it is for marketing, manufacturing, or finance.

The CIO is the natural focal point, that *single voice for IT*. As such, he or she is the company's internal and external communicator on IT matters. The CIO must be able to communicate in words, both written and spoken, as well as through behavior.

In many instances, behavior speaks louder than words. If the CIO is going to make the argument to other executive leaders that they do not need to have the latest and greatest toys, the CIO should not have them either. The CIO should not use the excuse that he or she is field testing these new technologies. If field testing is necessary, it should be done by the people in the field for whom the technology can offer the most help.

One business-unit CIO I worked with came to every meeting I attended with some new piece of "personal" technology gear. First, it was a lightweight laptop, then it was a personal digital assistant (PDA), and finally it was a next-generation wireless prototype that looked like something out of a movie. This CIO relished the opportunity to provide all of the business people at the meeting with a quick "show-and-tell" session. By the fourth meeting of this group, this CIO was being referred to as *Inspector Gadget*. When it came time to talk about ways of addressing some serious business issues, everyone had already tuned him out, assuming that his input was simply going to involve spending a lot of the company's money on some new IT toys. As smart as he was, that CIO could never free himself from the stereotype he had created.

A CIO who wishes to be seen by executive management peers as a true organizational leader and as worthy of a seat at the executive table needs to reach out to IT customers and other stakeholders. He or she needs not only to speak to them, but also, and more importantly, to listen to them. He or she must not only be able to say "No," but also, to say, "Let's talk about this and see how we can put a reasonable plan together."

WHAT SKILLS DOES THE NEW CIO NEED?

CASE STUDY 1.2
Skills of the New CIO

An engineering and construction services company that had been in business for many years had achieved only modest levels of organic growth. The company, however, was a high-quality "name" in the industry. As a family-owned and run organization, costs—including those for IT—had been a key focus. The CEO viewed IT more as a "tool" for his engineers to use in support of their work than as an enabler of increased growth within the business. Therefore, minimal investments were made in IT. The CEO appointed one of the company's top programmers to head up the IT Department. This individual's role was very simple and very clear: to focus on the individual applications and centralized infrastructure necessary to support what the engineers on the projects needed and to keep the costs down.

Because of an increase in global construction activity during the mid-1990s, the founder/owner of the company, who was approaching retirement age, concluded that the time was right to cash out. He began, therefore, to discuss the sale of the firm with a group of private investors. As the investors went through their due diligence efforts, they discovered a gold mine of opportunity based primarily on the company's significant potential for global growth, which included the possible acquisition of smaller construction and engineering companies. As part of its due diligence, the private investor group asked for an assessment of the current IT organization and its ability to enable and support the substantial level of anticipated growth. After only one day at the site, members of the group realized that the current head of IT was not up to the job that lay ahead. He was simply out of his league. He did not have the broad skills necessary to take IT to the next level and would not be able to play the important role of a business-oriented CIO.

The head of IT was still very valuable to the organization, and, to his credit, once the new CIO role was described to him, he quickly told the investor group that he would be happy to stay on, but only in the narrower role of systems development leader. He understood that the new CIO role required skills that were beyond his primarily technology-focused capabilities. Members of the investor group brought in an outside advisor to help them define the new CIO role to ensure that it would be focused appropriately on the needs of a company that was expected to double in size and significantly increase its profitability.

In defining the new CIO role, the advisor established four additional areas of skills concentration, beyond technology operations, that would be critical to success: (1) the ability to understand key business objectives and needs, (2) effective overall leadership and management capabilities, (3) a deep understanding of key organizational issues, and (4) the ability to deal with IT-related financial matters. The new CIO role was created, candidates were sourced, and the investor group selected the most appropriate candidate, who, ultimately, became a key player in helping to drive the growth and profitability the group had envisioned.

The skills necessary for leadership in the modern corporation can be divided into five types. Leaders today need skills in business, technology, leadership and management, organization and culture, and fiscal management. Leaders and managers in different functional areas of the business

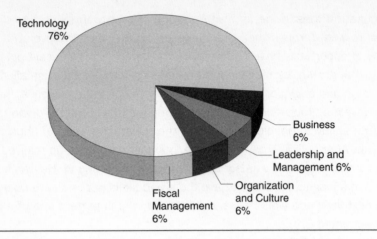

Figure 1.1   Allocation of Skills: CIOs and IT Directors.

have a need for greater or lesser skills in each of these five areas, but no effective leader can completely lack skills in any of the five.

The CIO of the twenty-first century needs very different skills than the CIO of previous generations. CIOs and IT directors from the 1970s through the 1990s had skills that were heavily skewed toward education and formal training in technology and engineering (Figure 1.1).

By comparison, the CIO of the twenty-first century needs a far more balanced set of skills (Figure 1.2).

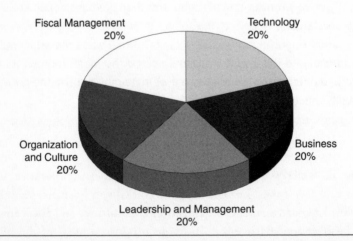

Figure 1.2   Balance of Skills Required for Today's CIO.

Business Skills

The CIO must know the company's business well enough to be able to assist concretely in the formulation of the company's business strategy and to identify key IT opportunities to help take that strategy forward. He or she must be able to blend into the corporate strategy the IT vision and strategy he or she has developed.

In addition, the CIO should have the ability and cross-cultural background necessary to assist in the development of region-based or business-unit-based business strategies and their parallel IT strategies. This can be achieved by working closely with regional or business-unit business leaders and IT heads.

Specific skills in the business group include understanding of:

- Companywide business strategies
- All business units and key linkages
- Global corporate issues.

Technology Skills

The CIO and his or her IT leadership team must be able to establish standards with regard to the selection, integration, and operations of complex IT solutions. In consultation with corporate and business-unit leaders, they should establish appropriate metrics and performance management systems to ensure adherence to the agreed-on standards.

The CIO also must have the skills necessary to plan and coordinate the development of a robust, flexible, and cost-effective network and telecommunications infrastructure.

Finally, the global CIO should direct research and evaluation of emerging and advanced technologies of interest to the company at the corporate or business-unit level. Although the CIO does not need to have in-depth knowledge of cutting-edge technology, he or she must be a "quick study," able to learn enough from the expert on staff who is watching the horizon to report intelligently on these technologies to the executive leadership team, business-unit leaders, and other constituencies.

Specific skills in the technology group include:

- Strategic-level knowledge of IT capabilities and emerging technologies
- Hands-on practical knowledge of implementation and rollout issues.

Leadership and Management Skills

Getting a seat at the corporate leadership table is not just a matter of being invited to sit down. To keep that seat, the CIO must be a true business leader. A big part of being a business leader is being able to facilitate communication about IT among worldwide business and IT leaders through regular contact, both in one-on-one and in group meetings, as well as in formal and informal written communications.

The CIO also must be able to lead the development of comprehensive business-line technology plans. Finally, managing relationships and other arrangements with vendors of both products and outsourced services is becoming a larger part of the CIO's management duties. This adds another level of relationship management and negotiating skills to those necessary to be a CIO.

Specific skills in the leadership and management group include:

- Executive presence
- Ability to work effectively at the board level
- Ability to transfer skills, knowledge, and best practices
- Willingness to be a visible, collegial, results-oriented player.

Organization and Culture Skills

CIOs need to manage the overall care and feeding of large groups of IT staff, often widely dispersed throughout the company. He or she must be able to resist the temptation to establish a military-like hierarchical organization and, instead, must focus on team building, skill development, and establishing a culture of trust.

In addition to earning the trust of executive management and business-unit leaders, the CIO must earn the trust of all members of the IT team, regardless of their roles. He or she should be viewed not just as the team leader—the "king" or "queen"—but also as a member of the team who, like any other team member, is held accountable for performance and results.

The day of the hierarchical IT leader is gone. Today's CIO must be able to build, lead, and be a working member of different teams within the IT organization, as well as work with cross-functional teams that include IT members. "Do as I say, not as I do," simply will not cut it any longer.

Specific skills in the organization and culture group include:

- Ability to understand human resources, organizational and behavioral issues, and change management techniques
- Ability to work within and across multiple, diverse cultures
- Ability to drive major organizational change.

Fiscal Management Skills

The CIO must be able to exercise appropriate fiscal management and control over the IT spend across the organization. He or she has fiduciary responsibility for all of the financial matters within IT, including the development and monitoring of IT budgets, the review and approval of IT expenditures, and the development and ongoing assessment of key financial and operational performance metrics within the IT organization.

As part of these responsibilities, the CIO should be held accountable for translating the implications of IT into financial terms with the appropriate level of transparency and clarity, in a way that the CFO and others on the executive management team can readily understand. This demands a set of skills far beyond the traditional project budgeting skills with which most past CIOs were comfortable.

Specific skills in the area of fiscal management include:

- Ability to work across business units and develop clear, business-focused IT budgets with appropriate transparency
- Ability to practically apply complex budgetary, portfolio management, financial management, and control concepts in an IT environment
- Understanding of business-driven IT and financial performance metrics, the impact they can have, and how to use them effectively to achieve desired behavioral changes.

WHAT ARE THE NEW CIO'S PRIMARY RESPONSIBILITIES?

The new CIO has primary responsibility in three areas:

1. People
2. Priorities
3. Performance.

People

Like today's CIO, members of the IT organization at all levels need to develop new skills. To facilitate this, the CIO must take responsibility for closely managing human resources, for recruiting a first-class human resources professional for the IT organization, and for establishing a career model for IT professionals, complete with performance and evaluation metrics, career path planning, and mentoring.

The CIO also needs to develop ways to cross-train IT professionals, exchange skills and capabilities on a global basis (both to facilitate transfer of best practices and to give IT staff members a chance to build their cultural competencies), and to rotate IT professionals into other business functions and operations.

Priorities

Today's CIOs must begin setting priorities by first establishing, and then living by, a set of key IT principles and by recognizing that change is the only constant they and their team members will ever know. They must be IT champions, demanding business ownership and accountability with regard to the constantly shifting IT priorities in a zero-sum game of fixed or declining IT expenditures.

The CIO must constantly wage the battle of focus in determining the few things that really count and in translating new and evolving business priorities into relevant, cost-effective IT actions. He or she also needs to understand that effective priorities cannot be set in an IT vacuum and that regular direct involvement and interaction with business-unit executives and users must be the norm.

Performance

The CIO as a businessperson should be the guardian of a range of IT business value metrics. These metrics must dynamically fit the current situation and contribute to desired outcomes, results, and improvements. The CIO's responsibility is to ensure the relevance of the IT business value metrics used, guiding the organization to the *focused few* instead of the unfocused many.

In addition, the CIO must ensure that everyone in the IT organization is focused on identifying the root causes of the problems they encounter and initiating the actions necessary to correct problems and improve processes.

Finally, today's CIO is also responsible for integrating all of the pieces of the IT puzzle. He or she must understand the impact on total costs downstream and not just deal with the individual pieces at discreet moments in time.

If used effectively, IT business value metrics will become one of the most important tools in the CIO's business management tool kit.

WHERE DOES THE NEW CIO RESIDE IN THE ORGANIZATION?

CASE STUDY 1.3
Situating the Role of the CIO within the Organization

The management board of a highly decentralized European-based food products company had recently decided to take advantage of economies and efficiencies made possible by new European Commission rules. They believed that because so many of their support operations and costs were spread throughout the continent, substantial savings could be achieved if they established a "Single Europe" concept and created shared services for all of these operations. IT was among the areas they believed they should address first. However, before they could grapple with IT, they had to deal with the fact that they had never had a corporate CIO (each of the decentralized companies had its own IT director).

As the board discussed the issue of establishing a corporate CIO position, they wrestled with the question of where to situate this role within the organization. The board recognized that bringing on a corporate CIO was going to be a major jolt to the organization (and especially to the company's IT directors). It also recognized that if IT were to be the first test of the Single Europe concept and the move toward shared services, the new CIO would have to be given some real authority within the company. However, accomplishing that objective meant ensuring that the corporate CIO position had "teeth" without alienating the local company IT directors, managing directors, and finance directors.

Because the management board consisted of key managing directors from various local companies as well as certain corporate directors, the board concluded that, at a minimum, the CIO must be a full member of the overall management board. That decision was easy. The board was split three ways with regard to the person to whom the corporate CIO should report. Some members felt the CIO should report to the corporate CEO, while others believed it should be the corporate finance director. Still others felt that the CIO should report to the full board, even though he or she was to be a member of the board. The board members could not agree. Those who wanted the CIO to report directly to the corporate CEO—the "power" group—felt that that solution would provide the CIO with maximum clout. Those who wanted the CIO to report to the finance director—the "control" group—believed that that solution would provide the best opportunity to control IT costs. Finally, those who believed that the CIO should report to the full board—the "fear" group—wanted to ensure that even though they would be the new CIO's peers, under this scenario, they could continue to have the most influence over the IT agenda.

The CEO allowed this dialogue to go on for quite some time before he weighed in on the issues. He clearly understood that the CIO needed the highest authority to get things done. Because this change would represent a major cultural shift for the company, the CEO expected a lot of resistance. He also realized that the local company managing directors needed to feel that they would be heard. However, he also had to ensure that other members of the management board would accept the CIO as a peer.

The key to the CEO's ultimate decision can be summed up in two words—access and balance. He had to balance the CIO's authority with full access. He accomplished this by making the CIO a full member of the management board with reporting responsibilities directly to CEO (hard line) and also to the local company managing directors (dotted line). As ambiguous as this structure might appear, it provided the CIO with the necessary top-management authority and clout and also held him accountable to the local company managing directors (his peers on the board). At the same time, this structure prevented the managing directors from exercising undue influence and allayed their fears. The organizational model proved to be successful and was subsequently used by the company in establishing other functional, shared services centers.

Lack of interest or understanding of technology, or, worse yet, fear of technology, causes many CEOs to run for cover at the prospect of the CIO's reporting directly to him or her. The myth that technology is nothing more than an administrative support function is perhaps the most compelling reason those destined to become CEOs do not feel they need to be competent in technology matters.

Another reason many CEOs do not want their CIO reporting directly to them is that historically, most CIOs have not done a very good job of communicating in ways that make CEOs comfortable. Thus, a CEO who is already less than conversant in technology does not want to demonstrate further public weakness (or possibly be humiliated) concerning IT should he or she fail to understand what the CIO is talking about (even though that may be entirely the CIO's fault).

The Korn/Ferry survey referenced earlier in this chapter queried CIOs about the importance of meeting regularly with the company's "C-level" leadership and asked them whether they sat on the company's executive leadership team.

With the CEO, German CIOs were most likely to meet at least weekly; 58 percent of German CIOs said they met either at least once a week or daily; 40 percent of American and French CIOs said they met either at least once a week or daily; and 26 percent of CIOs in the United Kingdom said they met either at least once a week or daily.

With the COO, French CIOs were most likely to meet at least weekly; 74 percent of French CIOs said they met either at least once a week or daily; 62 percent of CIOs in the United Kingdom met at least once a week, 46 percent of American CIOs met at least once a week; and 40 percent of German CIOs met at least once a week.

With the CFO, German CIOs were most likely to meet at least once a week; 71 percent of German CIOs met at least once a week; 62 percent of CIOs in the United Kingdom met at least once a week; 56 percent of French CIOs met at least once a week; and 55 percent of American CIOs met at least once a week.

These findings are summarized in Table 1.1.

While U.S. CIOs do not rank first in terms of interacting with any C-level executive on a regular basis, more U.S. CIOs sit on the their companies' executive committees. For example, 49 percent of U.S. CIOs sit on the executive committee while 36 percent of French and British CIOs and only 13 percent of German CIOs do so.

Further muddying the waters, 64 percent of American CIOs rated as "critically important" regular access to the CEO and other top corporate

Table 1.1 Percentage of CIOs Interacting Weekly or Daily with CEOs, COOs, and CFOs

	United States	United Kindgom	Germany	France
CEO	40	26	58	40
COO	46	62	40	74
CFO	55	62	71	56

executives, while only 46 percent of French, 31 percent of British, and 29 percent of German CIOs did so.

And finally, 84 percent of French CIOs and 74 percent of German CIOs recorded a high level of satisfaction with their relationships with other C-level executives, a larger percentage than either American or British CIOs.

These differences might possibly reflect the differences between European and American business organization, structure, and culture. But putting such differences aside, full and frequent communication is essential. I have seen many global teams disintegrate into an endless series of country/turf battles. However, in the majority of the cases, this did not occur because of any fundamental technology differences. The primary reason for these team failures was a lack of leadership and cultural sensitivity on the part of the CIO and his or her key lieutenants. The CIO must embrace and hone these skills as prerequisites to achieving any sort of success in the global arena.

WHAT THE CEO CAN DO TO HELP DEVELOP AND NURTURE THE NEW CIO

A CEO can take five concrete steps to help the company's CIO reach his or her full potential, both as a business executive and as the leader of an organization that is integral to the company's future success. The CEO can:

1. Recognize his or her own lack of interest in or fear of technology and admit that he or she needs to take the time to listen to someone with a business/technology focus and knowledge about IT matters.

2. Let the CIO into the executive club, make sure everyone else in the club is aware of this, create visible signs recognizing and accepting the importance of IT to the business, and consider IT as a business unit equal to the company's operating business units.

3. Help the CIO to communicate more effectively to the CEO and tell the CIO how he or she prefers written or verbal presentations to be made both in terms of structure and content. Most CIOs did not grow up in the traditional parts of the business—marketing, finance, and so on—that get people into the CEO's chair.

4. Move away from adherence to the myth that IT cannot be managed like any other business unit in the organization; expect performance measurements to be created that measure the business value of IT; and learn how the more discrete IT measurements are translated into business value metrics.

5. Establish ways to cut through the "fog" when he or she does not understand the CIO and use outside business-IT expertise as a sounding board to get a second, objective opinion about what the CIO is saying.

CHAPTER 2

Link IT Strategy to Corporate Strategy

The Chief Information Officer and Corporate Strategy

A global producer and distributor of novelty consumer goods had a history of failed IT projects. The company's IT management processes, controls, and accountability were limited, and its IT organization was totally out of step with company strategy.

A recent failure in implementation of the primary order management and distribution system had raised serious issues of concern to the new CEO and board about management of IT across the company. The head of IT had recently resigned, and a senior marketing executive from one of the business units was filling the position on an interim basis.

About to embark on a significant global strategy, top management wondered whether the company should establish a global CIO role and organization that would better link IT with corporate strategy. In addition, the CEO and board were keenly interested in ensuring that the company's IT structure, mission, and spend were consistent with the company's strategic objectives.

The company asked an outside firm to assess its worldwide IT organization in the context of the company's strategic growth plan and to assist in establishing a restructured IT organization more in line with the company's strategic business objectives and supported by improved IT management processes and controls surrounding resource and skills allocation, budgets, and key expenditures.

The outside experts focused on assessing the worldwide IT organization structure, IT resources, skills and capabilities, management processes, and overall portfolio. They interviewed business unit CEOs, other executives, and other users to determine their critical needs. They developed a pro forma global IT organization, including a CIO position, complete with role descriptions and key skills and characteristics of major players in the organization.

At the end of the exercise, executive management determined that hiring an executive-level CIO who would report directly to the CEO was critical to the success of corporate strategy. As a result of the analysis, the company's worldwide IT organization, resources, and capabilities were completely restructured to reflect evolving business needs. A global CIO was hired, and key IT management processes were implemented, including IT project prioritization and spending control processes.

Effective business planning is a team effort. Business leaders are responsible for developing the company's strategies, goals, and objectives, based on the focus of the business and its markets. The CIO should, at the same time, develop the technology strategies and tactics that will support and enhance each of the business goals. In addition, mutually agreed upon performance measurements need to be developed to track progress, identify gaps, and ensure alignment between IT and the business.

To do this effectively, the CIO needs to understand the entire corporate organization, the company's business objectives, and the current obstacles to achieving those objectives. In some instances, technology can be used to combat these obstacles; in other instances, these obstacles make some technology implementations irrelevant.

Companies that achieve such synergies and strongly forged ties between the CIO and other senior business leaders do so by developing a formal business planning process that fully integrates IT with the strategic business objectives of the entire organization.

Once such a plan is complete, both the CIO and the senior business leaders should be held accountable for how well the technology contributes to business value. Some companies go so far as to have the business units propose technology initiatives that map to their needs. Then, when the technology is deployed, they are held accountable for its success or failure.

This approach may not work for every company. However, all companies should set expectations during planning so that all business units understand how involved they will be in measuring the value of their individual technology solutions.

"It used to be that the CIO's career was defined by his technical competence. Today and in the future, a CIO's role and success are and will be defined by the skills of networking, influence, and business acumen, in addition to the traditional accountability for delivering the technology vision and strategy. By diligently tying IT investments to business goals and strategy, CIOs can ensure that their companies understand and appreciate technology as a resource that can be leveraged for competitive advantage. As they succeed in that mission, the role of the CIO will continue to evolve and grow in stature and importance."*

DEVELOPING THE IT STRATEGIC PLAN

Developing an IT strategy is a process, not an event. It involves a logical set of steps that leads to an outcome that can be accepted by corporate and business-unit leadership as well as by the IT organization. Because IT strategy development occurs in a constantly shifting and changing environment, the process must be dynamic and continuous. The best IT strategy is constantly being refreshed and adjusted to reflect changing business and market conditions, as well as evolving technology issues.

An IT strategy must be written in language that everyone can understand. It must be rigorously tied to the company's business objectives and business strategy. It should be limited to three-to-seven strategic imperatives that the IT organization must accomplish to enable the company to meet its business objectives.

The process of IT strategic development must take into account the business context in which the company works. One of the CIO's key roles is to keep the CEO and business-unit executives from signing off on wasteful IT expenditures. Therefore, every suggestion for an IT enhancement must be looked at through the context filter of the company's situation, its business objectives, and its competitive environment.

---

* Chris Lofgren, "The Importance of Being Influential," *CIO* (March 15, 2003). Available at www.cio.com/archive/031503/perspective.html.

For instance, a biosciences company looking to skinny itself down into a pharmaceutical company by divesting itself of animal care products and basic chemicals needs a totally different kind of IT strategy than an entertainment company that needs to digitize much of its content to deliver it on a pay-per-use basis or a catalog sales company that is moving into retail sales.

The process of developing an IT strategic plan involves considering hundreds or even thousands of ideas expressed by people throughout the organization concerning what they want to do with technology and choosing to act on those that are most important, financially feasible, and acceptable in terms of risk.

As Anna Danilenko, IDC Consulting Services Program Manager, puts it, "The most important trends with regard to IT investment going forward include a greater focus on optimizing existing IT systems as opposed to investing in new initiatives, the need for aligning the business and IT strategies, and a holistic approach to business and IT problems, renewing focus on ROI [return on investment] and financial validation concerning IT investments. This translates into the need for CIOs to become far more effective in managing their IT organizations in a more fiscally intense and business-like manner."

The six steps of the IT strategy development process are:

1. Understanding the business strategy
2. Identifying IT vision
3. Determining IT strategic objectives
4. Analyzing the portfolio of IT initiatives
5. Preparing the IT strategic plan
6. Regularly refreshing the IT vision and/or plan as needed.

As illustrated in Figure 2.1, the first step in the IT strategic plan is carried out by the corporate leadership team, with input from the CIO. Steps two through five are executed by the CIO and IT organizational leaders, with input from other corporate and business-unit leaders. The sixth step, periodic refreshment of the IT vision and plans, takes place when needed, but at least once a year during the annual planning process.

In the real world, however, these steps are not always carried out in sequence. The actions they involve are not point-in-time discrete activities.

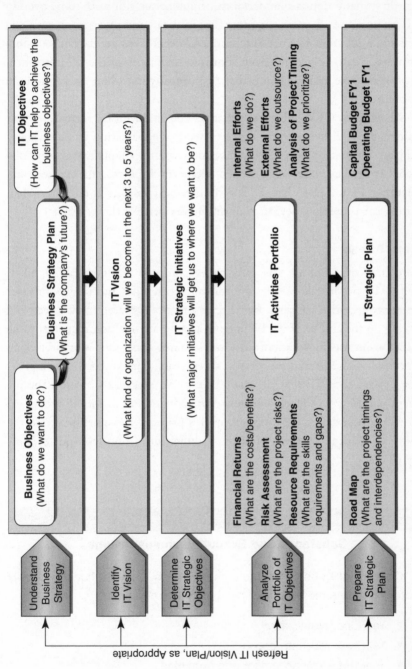

Figure 2.1 Overview of Information Technology Strategy Process.

41

In reality, many steps are undertaken simultaneously or with some overlap or flow into one another; some steps are initiated and then reviewed as the results of a previous step are finalized; and other steps are carried out on a continuous basis (e.g., real-time continuous analysis of the IT portfolio). But for the sake of discussion, the steps are discussed here as stand-alone procedures.

I have seen CIOs tell CEOs that, in the absence of a formal written business plan, they could not move forward with creating an IT strategy and plan. I also have seen CIOs create multivolume IT plans that were obsolete before they were even finished. However, following the six steps and executing a good plan that is 75 to 85 percent complete is far better than waiting to complete a perfect plan that never gets off the ground.

Keep IT Lean

More than ever before, the only thing constant about corporate IT is change. IT product life cycles are forever shortening, and business strategies are constantly changing. For this reason, an IT strategy that is lean and focused on the ability of the IT organization to act in a way that adds value to the business is more important than a strategy that says X will be done in two years and Y will be done in three years. The key is to put a planning process in place that fits the business and takes into account the inherent volatility in today's business environment and in the IT world. At the end of the day, the IT organization's primary mission should be the ability to manage the ever-present combination of business and technology change.

CASE STUDY 2.2
Substance and Execution versus Volume

One new CIO who came into a chaotic IT environment had an initial IT strategy that was merely three lines on a piece of paper:

- Year one: stabilization
- Year two: reconstruction
- Year three: enhancement and execution.

During the first year, while he was working to stabilize the IT environment, he used his seat at the table to grill his executive colleagues about how the IT organization and infrastructure should be reconstructed. Before the beginning of year two, he had written an agreed-to plan with specific guidance about what the reconstruction would look like and how the enhancement should proceed in year three.

Understanding Business Strategy

Before a company can make effective IT investments, senior management must paint a clear picture of where it intends to lead the business. Any effective information technology strategy must be based on the answers to key strategic questions.

Often, the business strategy and IT strategy are developed simultaneously, playing off each other in an effort to capture the dynamics of internal and external forces.

The business strategy answers the question: "What is the company's future?" To get there, executives need to ask what they want from the business and how IT can help them achieve their various business objectives. To formulate the right questions, the CEO and the leadership team need to define the gaps that exist between the current business and technology strategies.

To establish a business strategy that can realistically leverage the company's technology, the leadership team should review available business and technology plans, conduct an IT performance appraisal and identify opportunities for improvement, and develop scenarios to test the robustness of business and technology assumptions. At the same time, they should be identifying gaps in current performance and future needs. IT cannot be an afterthought or add-on to the business strategy development process. In today's business world, where technology is woven into so many business processes, IT must be integral and inseparable from business strategy.

Integrating IT strategy with the business strategy encourages IT business-unit and corporate executives to take ownership of the strategy and discourages them from considering IT to be a *free* service. Marrying IT to the business strategy forces business unit and corporate leaders to negotiate IT investments with the aim of supporting various business lines, product lines, or regional businesses in the same way that they negotiate other budgetary items.

It is essential, however, that the CIO not wait for the leather-bound document titled "Business Strategy" to arrive before acting. Although formal business planning initiatives are appropriate (and beyond the scope of this book), the CIO needs a visceral understanding of the company's strategy; and the CEO and other executives need to make sure they keep the CIO apprised of changes over time that can affect that strategy and IT's place within it.

A CIO who lacks confidence or who is timid about moving forward without having a formally signed, ironclad business strategy document in hand is demonstrating that he or she really does not understand the business well enough, does not have the executive-level skills of a business–unit leader, and lacks the senior-level relationships necessary to take appropriate calculated IT business risks. I have known many CIOs who have not been willing to step out and take the risks necessary to drive breakthrough ideas forward in their organizations. Some of these are now former CIOs, and the rest have become technology *caretakers* rather than participants at the executive table.

Case Study 2.3

Flexibility versus Formality

A COO of a company in the media and communications industry that was undergoing dramatic change and corporate turmoil brought in an outside IT advisor.

Sales of the company's products were strong, but start-up competitors were rapidly building a new, technology-based business model involving electronic distribution vehicles and the digitization of media content.

While this was going on, the company's CIO was tightly and proudly clutching his three-year IT plan developed more than a year earlier, insisting that if the COO and other senior executives could not provide him with a definitive new business strategy, he would have no choice but to follow his old plan because "the discipline of even a somewhat outdated plan outweighs the risks of allowing too much experimentation with new technology . . ."

In truth, the industry's rapidly evolving business models made it impossible for business executives to create a traditional, static business strategy document.

What the CIO should have done was to immerse himself, together with the business-unit leaders and other executives, into the issues at hand and work together to understand the impact of the new business model on their respective businesses. At the same time, they should have been creating a real-time IT strategic direction that would reprioritize, refocus, add, and delete key IT expenditures and initiatives.

The COO determined that the CIO was a dinosaur and decided to dismiss him. He brought in the IT advisor to help define the CIO's role more clearly and to delineate the qualities and characteristics he should look for in the search for the new CIO.

Identifying IT Vision

CASE STUDY 2.4

Integrating IT Strategy with Company Spend Plans

Executives at a large American financial services company were concerned about not getting value from IT spending. They sought guidance on how future technology spending should be allocated and were particularly interested in exploring opportunities not only to reduce technology spending, but also to leverage existing technology and implement best practices, including targeted outsourcing. These efforts were aimed at better meeting the firm's business strategy.

An outside expert conducted an independent review and assessment of existing technology investments. He benchmarked the firm's spending against comparable companies, using proprietary databases focused on IT staffing, cost allocations, organizational structure, knowledge management, IT priorities, security, and a host of other relevant metrics.

Recommendations included development of a rigorous IT strategy, better internal communication for IT, a new governance model, risk reduction, cost visibility, and resource optimization, among other issues. As a result, the firm's management was better prepared to integrate IT spending with the firm's strategy, using an approach that promoted IT management credibility and firmwide accountability for IT strategy and portfolio management.

As the strategic business plan is being put into place, the IT team can go to work on its part of the IT strategic plan. The business plan is often not being driven by IT realities. Part of the IT strategic plan development, therefore, is to create a vision to get the IT organization mobilized to develop a technology environment that enables the company to implement the corporate business strategy, even if the business strategy does not articulate the technology component.

Sometimes this means dropping past plans, canceling projects, or reordering projects that had been on the planning horizon. It might mean rationalizing the technology infrastructure or implementing cutting-edge technologies. At other times, it means doing all of these things together.

Once the IT leadership team has identified the organization's vision, it must then communicate that vision throughout the IT organization and to the IT organization's various constituencies, both at the corporate and business-unit levels.

As illustrated in Figure 2.2, this exercise is no different from any other business/risk portfolio exercise performed every day by executives evaluating all types of business investments and expenditures.

CASE STUDY 2.5
Enabling Results by Linking IT to Company Strategy

Executives at a company with two primary businesses—one in electronic consumer goods and the other in information services—asked an outside consultant to review the effectiveness of the company's existing global IT budget, including overall technology spending of $110 million annually, and to help develop a portfolio-based, three-year IT strategic plan, the annual operating plans, and the supporting IT management processes.

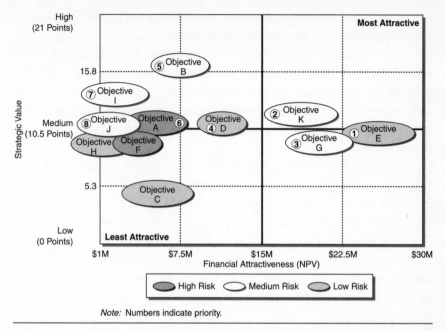

Figure 2.2   IT Objective Attractiveness Matrix.

Cost analysis, identification of opportunities for effective IT spending, and establishment of business-focused priorities were important components of this strategy and planning work.

The company had a history of failed IT projects. Senior management perceived that too much had historically been spent on IT, with too little to show for it. The business units supported by the technology were not engaged in a dialogue about their objectives and how IT should be used as an enabler of those objectives.

The new CEO considered technology to be an integral part of the businesses and appointed a new CIO who, in turn, sought help in understanding current IT spending and sorting through the right priorities for IT spending. Management believed there were important opportunities for more effective use of IT resources and assets and even for possible cost reduction—hence, the CIO's request for an outside analysis.

The outside expert worked with the CIO to establish a business-focused, portfolio management approach to sorting out IT priorities. They started with a baseline understanding of where the company was spending money on IT and helped the company focus on the highest value spending from the standpoint of supporting the business units.

This involved understanding IT's contribution to the business units, which had been intermittent and contentious in the past, and creating a process to start a dialogue between IT and the business units. The consultant then helped the CIO with portfolio analysis and budgeting, providing discipline and structure that enabled the CIO to sort through and get to the business cases for IT spending.

This work and the IT management processes put in place led to the business-unit leaders reaching agreement on IT priorities and to the creation of a detailed, pragmatic, and dynamic view of key IT initiatives and objectives. It also led to the development of clear, business-focused, and flexible action plans.

The entire process also considerably enhanced the credibility of the new CIO and helped to educate the business-unit leaders as to how IT could be directly integrated into their business plans and become a key enabler to achieve results.

Determining IT Strategic Objectives and Initiatives

The end product of this effort is a full description of all of the current IT initiatives that can move the company toward meeting its business objectives and achieving its business strategy. These initiatives must be ranked, both in order of importance and according to which are most achievable from a technical perspective. Ranking according to level of importance depends heavily on honest input from corporate and business-unit leaders, whereas the technical ranking is driven by the IT organization's skills and knowledge.

Corporate, business-unit, and IT leaders must be brutally honest when developing these rankings. Ranking as a *must have* something that is technologically difficult but only *nice to have* forces the IT organization to put maximum effort into the project, draining resources from other, more important initiatives. I worked with an executive management group that was unable to make the tough calls on IT priorities, using the "We're not technology people" excuse. The result was that more than 800 IT requests sat in the queue, all having the same priority—high. This effectively allowed the company's real business priorities ultimately to be decided by the technology staff, who simply worked their way through the 800 requests, responding in ways they thought made the most sense.

CASE STUDY 2.6
Analyzing the Portfolio of IT Initiatives

A North American- and European-based global information services company had embarked on a strategic plan to achieve significant growth in its core businesses by making numerous acquisitions of U.S. companies or business units over a relatively short period of time. Despite this aggressive plan, executive management wished to avoid creating a huge, bureaucratic, centralized corporate infrastructure. A small corporate group, made up of a chairman, a CEO, a CFO, and some key accounting, tax, and legal resources formed the core of the "acquisition engine," drawing expert resources from inside and outside the company as needed.

To complete preacquisition financial, operational, and IT due diligence efforts and to drive postdeal integration efforts, corporate management engaged outside advisors on a regular basis over a period of years.

In the IT realm, this work involved rapidly evaluating each acquisition target company's IT organization, capabilities, management processes, overall spend, and current portfolio of IT investments. It also involved helping to determine deal price and future reserve impact to bring the technology up to the standard necessary to achieve the parent company's strategic objectives.

Historically, IT had not been a major focus of the company's acquisition due diligence. Most deals were centered on the fit of the target company and its ability to fuel strategic growth within a specific market segment, as well as on the financial implications of the deal. Operational matters, including IT, were often left until the financial deal had been completed.

However, in the latter half of the 1990s, as IT began to gain increasing importance in the information and publishing industry, corporate management realized the need for IT to have a seat at the table in preacquisition due diligence. IT due diligence, especially in *market-defining* as opposed to niche-market acquisitions, was often a substantial consideration. In many cases, the state of the target company's technology became the focal point for acquisition negotiations and for pricing the deal primarily because information technology took on more of a manufacturing plant and distribution mechanism role in the information services industry as downloading from databases replaced the printing and mailing of paper copies.

Over time, detailed models were developed for IT spend analysis, strategic IT prioritization, IT organizational assessment, IT budgeting, IT investment portfolio development, and IT functional capabilities as they pertained to the information and publishing industry. This allowed the company more cost effectively to conduct due diligence, to negotiate price based on real information about the IT assets it was acquiring and on whether they would be abandoned or become the core for a group of similar businesses, and to integrate acquisitions into the enterprise more easily.

The approach to developing IT strategy, in this case, tracked very closely with how the business was being run and how it ultimately evolved—from a lean-and-mean, run-and-gun philosophy to a far more traditional, albeit still highly entrepreneurial, divisional organization.

Another layer of analysis must be undertaken before IT leadership can determine which initiatives (and, therefore, which objectives) should be included in the strategic plan.

Initiatives should be weighed against six criteria:

1. *Term:* short to long
2. *Risk:* low to high
3. *Size/scale:* small to large
4. *Scope:* local to global
5. *Cost:* low to high
6. *Need: got-to-have* to *great-to-have.*

Figure 2.3 illustrates the stages of technology support for business initiatives. It is important to understand where the company's IT initiatives sit on this continuum at the present and where the company would like its IT initiatives to sit in the future. This helps determine how much risk needs to be undertaken in the overall portfolio.

The portfolio should be balanced in these six criteria; implementing only *safe initiatives* (i.e., low cost, low risk, short term, local) places the company at risk of being routed by competitors, whereas implementing only *risky initiatives* (i.e., high cost, high risk, long term, global) puts the company at

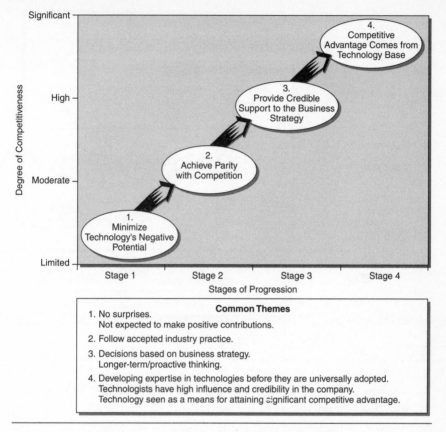

Figure 2.3   Stages of Technology Support.

risk of experiencing catastrophic IT failure. The portfolio of IT initiatives can be mapped on a matrix such as that illustrated in Figure 2.4.

In developing the portfolio, six major factors need to be considered:

1. *Financial impact:* What are the costs and benefits?
2. *Risk assessment:* What are the specific risks associated with the spend item or initiative?
3. *Resource requirements:* What are the skills required to execute the initiative, and what are the gaps in present IT organization skills?
4. *Internal efforts:* What is the company capable of executing internally with the requisite quality?

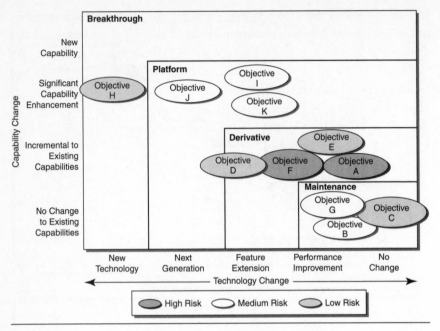

Figure 2.4   IT Internal Impact Matrix.

5. *External efforts:* To what extent would the company consider out-sourcing certain aspects of the portfolio?
6. *Timing:* What are the time frame constraints or commitments for the spend item or initiative?

Thorough assessment of the financial impact of any spend item or initiative included in the portfolio is essential. The assessment must take into consideration the total costs and benefits (not just the costs within the IT organization and function) from a total IT spend perspective. In evaluating the relative risks of a portfolio item, risk factors such as competition, benefits predictability, regulatory requirements, planning predictability, IT capability, operations reliability, and technology positioning need to be considered.

Existing skills in the IT organization must be compared with the skills necessary to undertake each initiative. If a major overhaul in organizational skills is necessary, it may not be possible to undertake all of the initiatives desired within the plan's time frame because of the extra time and management energy involved in recruiting and training new personnel and in retooling of existing personnel whose skills are no longer needed. Sometimes this analysis leads to a decision to reorganize the IT organization. One company I worked with was spending 95 percent of its IT budget just on keeping the wind in the sails and on maintaining the organization's aging systems and infrastructure. When management finally decided that it was time to reprioritize and to focus on new technologies to reduce their overall IT spend, they realized that it would take at least a year longer than they had planned to reorganize. They now had to bring in completely new skills and to totally retool their existing staff.

Alternatively, outsourcing may be a way either to acquire new skills or to support old technologies while new skills are acquired. Or, management can simply buy those new skills "by the pound" through some sort of a utility-like outsourcing arrangement.

A company that does not want to put the time or resources into developing cutting-edge IT skills can search for a strategic outsourcing partner. A company that finds itself using much of its IT human resources merely to manage legacy systems may find that outsourcing those systems allows the development of cutting-edge skills that can be used to implement and utilize forward-looking IT. Some skills can be rapidly acquired through selective use of outside consulting or outsourcing arrangements.

Finally, the issue of timing needs to be considered as a key factor in determining the relative priority of the portfolio item.

CASE STUDY 2.7

Making IT a Contributor during the Acquisition Process

A manufacturer of electrical parts in the United States and Europe sought to expand its product line and customer list by acquiring all or part of a competitor with seven different business units. Complicating the due diligence analysis was the fact that many elements of the business process support structure, including IT, were shared to varying degrees by the business units.

Inclusion of various combinations of business units in the acquisition would have a major impact on the costs that would be incurred disentangling the IT environment. Needing to complete the acquisition in a timely manner, the company asked an outside advisor to review the target company's IT infrastructure and to determine the most appropriate mix of IT spend and initiatives that would comprise its portfolio going forward. This included:

- Actual degree to which IT and/or business process support was intermingled across business units
- Degree of interconnectivity with customers and suppliers in each business unit
- Integration of IT strategy with overall business-unit strategy
- Adequacy of the current and planned IT budgets to support current and future needs of each business unit
- Adequacy of systems (hardware and software) to support a number of key business processes, including: (1) product development and engineering, (2) marketing, (3) quoting/estimating, (4) order entry, (5) material requirement planning, (6) distribution/logistics, (7) general accounting and financial reporting, (8) purchasing and accounts payable, (9) billing and accounts receivable, and (10) payroll and benefits administration
- Appropriateness of the IT organization's size and skills to support current and future needs
- Adequacy of business continuity plans
- Relative costs, timing, and priority of each category of ongoing IT spend and each initiative.

As a result of this portfolio analysis of current strengths and weaknesses in the IT organization, its ongoing management, and its future initiatives, the company was able to more accurately assess transition costs and establish a more realistic negotiating position and complete the acquisition of the units that provided the most value to the business.

Equally important, the company was able to integrate elements of the target's IT portfolio in a cost-effective and timely manner and to determine the overall impact.

Preparing the IT Strategic Plan

Once the IT strategy has been agreed to, the plan needs to be constructed with appropriate implementation plans and metrics. The strategic initiatives that are part of the plan are finalized, in their order of rank, taking into account importance, achievability, cost, and risks.

A plan is then developed to accommodate changes in the skills base of the IT organization and how these changes will be implemented. Timetables and interdependencies are documented to gauge progress and assist in any root-cause analysis of implementation problems.

The documented plan itself is simply the physical manifestation of the result of the extensive prioritization, negotiation, and portfolio analysis work that has already taken place.

CASE STUDY 2.8

Periodically Refreshing the Vision and Plan

A mid-size, full-service European bank had a history of failed IT projects. Executives were concerned about excessively high IT service delivery costs and about an infrastructure comprised of disparate systems that required workarounds to ensure consolidation and reconciliation of key data. The CIO resigned under pressure, and the board of directors asked an outside advisor to assist in identifying more effective operating models for IT in support of the bank's strategic direction.

The advisor collected IT spend information as well as end-user satisfaction ratings and benchmarked these against other similar-size financial institutions. In addition, business priorities were assessed versus current IT priorities, and a new IT portfolio was established that focused on the implementation of new IT service management processes and restructuring of the IT organization to ensure better support of the bank's business strategy. Because of the work, the bank was in a position to move forward with a plan to optimize its IT service delivery and cost structure, thus improving its competitiveness.

Developing an IT strategy is not a one-time, static exercise or event. It must become a continuous, dynamic, actively managed process. The IT strategy itself must be refreshed regularly almost to the point of becoming a real-time document.

Years ago, some CIOs attempted to develop 10-year IT strategies. Although that may have seemed appropriate in a world where companies operated off one large mainframe, the folly of trying to predict so far into the future soon became obvious.

Few, if any, CIOs today prepare plans for more than three years into the future. The pace of change has accelerated greatly; 18-month product cycles are no longer the exception in either hardware or software. Add to that the rate of business change coming about through mergers, acquisitions, divestitures, and joint ventures, and it is clear that IT plans need to be revisited at least as frequently as the routine business-planning cycle, if not more frequently due to the particular circumstances of the business.

Even with the best of plans, everyone knows that market forces and events of the day often take control, dictating dramatic changes to IT organizational priorities. For this reason, the best way to plan for IT is actually to *plan for change*. A military analogy might clarify the point. The twenty-first century IT organization needs to have a large component of practitioners who operate more like special forces in the military than the regular service. And the rest of the IT organization needs to have developed the flexibility to fill in for these special forces when they are called on to surround and deal with a particular IT issue that has become a top priority.

WHAT THE CEO CAN DO TO HELP LINK IT STRATEGY TO BUSINESS STRATEGY

A CEO can take five concrete steps to ensure that the company's IT strategy is an integral part of the overall business strategy rather than a planning afterthought. The CEO can:

1. Recognize that IT strategy development is a continuous, dynamic process rather than a point-in-time, static event; that this process is inextricably linked to the overall business strategy; and that IT strategy is affected by market forces and other external factors as well as by internal corporate forces.
2. Require that the IT strategy be prepared in business terms rather than in technical terms and that the content of the IT strategy be simple, easy for nontechnical people to understand, and flexible enough to

address changing needs. The key to a good IT strategy is substance, focus, and business relevance, not the level of technical detail included.

3. Encourage the CIO to live and walk in the shoes of business-unit leaders. If the CIO does not have prior business-unit operating experience, the CEO should arrange for the CIO to do a mini tour in each business to learn the ropes (e.g., spend a week with a sales team, a week with field service, a week shadowing a plant manager, and a week answering customer service calls). This will help the CIO understand how real users interact with the technology the organization is managing and help to open the CIO's eyes to the need for real-world IT solutions as opposed to IT *elegance*.

4. Not sign off on the IT strategy unless the IT spend and initiatives are examined, assessed, and presented as a full IT portfolio, including total costs, quantitative and qualitative benefits, and key business risks.

5. Make sure he or she fully understands how each major IT spend item advances the business strategy or takes care of a particular tactical problem. If that understanding and linkage is not clear, the CEO should hold the line and be prepared to say no to the IT strategy.

CHAPTER 3

IT Management Is about Relationship Management

<table><tr><td>CASE STUDY 3.1</td></tr></table>

Relationships Make a Difference

A private equity firm was seeking to invest in a large, U.S.-based multilevel marketing company with global operations. The target company's management realized that its IT infrastructure was unstable. It was not uncommon for the firm's mission critical systems to crash, affecting hundreds of users for half a day or more. Orders could not be taken, processed, or shipped, creating angry customers and system users.

The target company's CIO had been terminated recently because of his inability to work with business leaders and his failure to complete prior IT projects aimed at improving the business's effectiveness. The CFO, working with two internal IT staff members, had charted a path to replace the company's unstable legacy systems over an 18-month period at a cost of $36 million. Senior management was fully committed to the upgrade plan.

As part of its due diligence related to acquiring the company, the private equity firm sought an independent opinion of the reasonableness of the target company's IT plan and of the current state of the IT operations. The kind of rapport that developed between the outside advisor and the target company's CEO and CFO had been missing between the target company's former CIO and executive management. The former CIO's inability to establish effective working relationships and communications with the company's business-unit leaders led to significant business problems and to the CIO's dismissal.

Because of the relationship between the outside advisors and the target company's executive leadership, the advisors were able to guide company executives to take the necessary actions to put the IT plan back on track. In addition, the advisors helped them understand that when they next looked to hire a CIO, they would need to ensure that one of the key criteria would be the candidate's ability to establish and maintain good working relationships with corporate and business-unit leadership.

Because of the advisor's work, leadership of both the target company and the private equity firm realized that:

- The $36 million cost estimate had been significantly understated.
- The target company was not likely to remain viable using its existing unstable legacy systems. The new system would need to be brought online.
- Business risk could be significantly reduced by stabilizing the legacy systems, and a feasible approach was available.

The acquisition was completed. The legacy system was stabilized, and the new infrastructure was implemented more gradually than previously planned. Over time, the target company also hired a new CIO.

The CIO of a large, complex corporation wears four different hats:

1. *Business executive for the IT organization,* managing a staff of technical and business professionals and support people in an organization that can range in size from a few dozen individuals to several thousand
2. *Technology business strategist,* creating the information technology strategy that is fully integrated with the business strategy
3. *Technology business advisor to the board and executive leadership team,* working on a day-to-day basis with other corporate leaders to keep them up to speed about how technology affects and is affected by every business decision they make
4. *IT architect and operator,* making the final decisions about the technology architecture to be put in place to maximize business decisions and optimize IT investments to create shareholder value and provide ongoing quality service to technology users.

Because of these four distinct yet related roles, the CIO has to manage several different relationships, each of which requires a different set of interaction, relationship management, and communication skills.

These various constituencies and skills include:

- *Peers on the executive management team:* These individuals should be educated about the role of the information technology organization, the appropriate use of information technology, and the role they can play in making IT a strategically enabling factor for the company.
- *Business-unit CEOs:* These individuals are, in many ways, the main constituents of the IT organization's main-line service delivery and project efforts, and the CIO must work closely with them to ensure that expectations on all fronts are met.
- *Technology users:* Everyone who uses any kind of technology is a "customer" and a recipient of day-to-day IT services.
- *Members of the corporate CIO organization:* The CIO needs not only to educate these individuals about their role in a high-powered service delivery organization, but also to lead them and shape them into a customer-oriented team. Also, the CIO often must run interference for them when customers need help in understanding realistic expectations.
- *Business-unit CIOs and business-unit information technology organization members:* These individuals must balance the demands of two masters: corporate IT and business-unit executive management.
- *IT staff throughout the organization:* These individuals are looking to the CIO to provide leadership and a sense of whether the CIO is interested in their continued career development.
- *Outside vendors of hardware, software, or services:* As much as possible, the corporate CIO should be the point of contact for these providers.

PERSON IN THE MIDDLE

One of the key roles of a CIO is to be the person in the middle of these various constituencies (Figure 3.1), acting as a buffer between them so they do not come into direct conflict with each other.

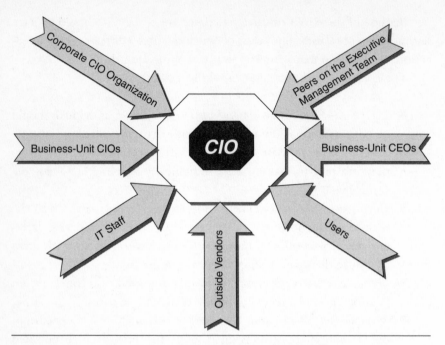

Figure 3.1   CIO: Person in the Middle.

As Stan Lepeak, Vice President, Professional Services Strategies, for META Group says, "Knowledge sharing and communications are crucial to the success of business units and IT organizations alike. Knowledge sharing is not about IT; it is about how people interact and build relationships with one another, and share ideas and best practices. Technology is the engine that drives an organization's ability to more easily build relationships, but the success of relationship building and knowledge sharing is dependent upon a culture within the company that encourages, supports, and rewards such behavior. In such organizations, when IT staff help users solve technical problems, they are focused on the ultimate goal of the users and the business, not just the technology."

The CIO needs to act as a shock absorber for each of these various constituencies, mediating and arbitrating the various needs of each constituency to make sure that technology efforts are consistent and in the best interests of the company. This does not always involve making decisions. In fact, the CIO may make few business decisions about IT investments. Instead of making these decisions, a skilled CIO explains the conflicts inherent in competing requests for IT resources and places the burden back on business-unit and corporate leadership teams to work out the specifics. In a sense, the CIO becomes the ultimate facilitator and mediator; this requires skills in negotiation, leadership, communication, and relationship management.

To be effective in this role, the CIO must be respected as a business executive by the corporate and business-unit leadership teams and must have developed strong working relations with the various constituents who compete for the CIO's time and energy and with the financial and human resources of the IT organization. Without effective and credible relationships, the CIO will not be able to play this role.

The number and nature of relationships that must exist between a CIO and his or her IT organization and other individuals and organizations within and outside the company are many and often complex. The most common of these relationships are illustrated in Figure 3.2.

In addition, numerous types of interactions must occur between the CIO and members of the IT organization and other individuals and organizations within and outside the company.

Table 3.1 illustrates the level of responsibility for technology planning that various individuals have in relation to one another.

All of these interactions are critical to an effective technology planning process. Having direct responsibility to every other constituency, the CIO has an enormous challenge in building and maintaining effective relationships throughout the company. For today's CIO, accomplishing this complex challenge is critical to success.

A company I worked with over a period of seven years brought in at least five externally recruited CIOs during that time frame. A primary reason for this embarrassing and disruptive CIO revolving door was the inability of each of these CIOs to understand the critical need to build effective, trust-based relationships throughout all segments of the company. As a result, the IT organization was unable to fulfill its fundamental mission. What finally turned the situation around was the appointment of a CIO from a business-unit operating role within the company. Because this individual already had extensive personal relationships throughout the company, she was able to hit the ground running in IT by effectively using and leveraging her extensive network of relationships and her understanding of the company.

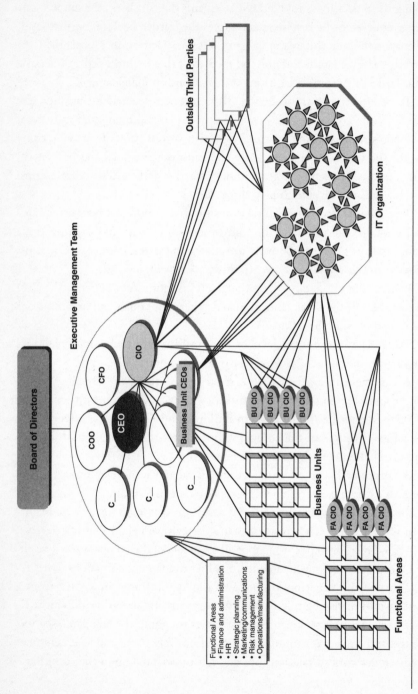

Figure 3.2 CIO/IT Organization Relationships Overview.

Table 3.1 Technology Planning Relationship Matrix

Group	Group Mission/Objective	Board of Directors	CEO	Business-Unit CEOs	Functional Area Leaders	Business-Unit CIOs	Functional Area IT Leaders	Outside Third Parties	IT Organization	CIO
Board of directors	Corporate oversight.	■	D	I	I	A	A	N	A	D
CEO	Development and execution of corporate strategy.	D	■	I	I	A	A	N	I	D
Business-unit CEOs	Development and execution of business-unit strategies/operations.	I	I	■	I	D	I	N	I	D
Functional area leaders	Development and execution of functional area strategies/operations.	I	I	I	■	I	D	N	I	D
Business-unit CIOs	Run IT operations for business units.	A	A	D	I	■	A	I	D	D
Functional area IT leaders	Run IT operations for functional areas.	A	A	I	D	D	■	I	D	D
Outside third parties	Provide outsourced services.	N	N	N	N	A	I	■	D	D
IT organization	Deliver quality IT services to all users in the company.	A	I	D	I	A	D	D	■	D
CIO	Develop and execute IT strategies/operations linked to business.	D	D	D	D	D	D	D	D	■

Key:
D - Direct and continuous responsibility
I - Intermittent responsibility
A - As needed
N - None

Example for Illustrative Purposes Only

65

BUILDING RELATIONSHIPS ONE AT A TIME

A CIO cannot be expected to come into a struggling IT organization and immediately turn it around. He or she needs time and a personal strategy to begin creating an organization that is high performing, focused on results, and responsive to users and that does not pander to every individual's whim. In other words, the CIO must develop a firm but fair and balanced approach to managing day-to-day workflow and one-off projects.

The relationships the CIO focuses on building first are determined by the company's corporate culture, the management style of the CEO and business-unit leaders, the *mental health* of the IT organization, and the role IT should play in making the company successful.

It is very difficult to be prescriptive about how to accomplish this objective. What follows, however, illustrates how one CIO created a set of relationships over time that transformed a chaotic IT situation into a focused, forward-looking organization.

CASE STUDY 3.2

Relationships Are the Cornerstones of Successful IT Organizations

In the mid-1990s, a new CIO was named for a large, U.S.-based media services company with numerous offices around the world. The company's new—and first—CIO was, by training, a business executive and not a technologist.

A new management team brought with it a new vision and mission: to achieve substantial revenue growth in key areas. In addition, the leadership team was committed to streamlining and upgrading the capabilities of four key internal corporate functions: accounting, human resources, operations, and IT.

Of the four, IT was the most troubled. Although substantial investments in IT had been made over the years, results had been inconsistent. Two separate IT organizations existed, one providing services to the corporate functions and another to the service professionals who dealt with customers. Staffing the second group were hundreds of individuals spread out around the world, each making individual IT infrastructure and support decisions.

IT directors led parts of the organization, while technical IT support people were hired locally and reported to their local office's senior management, most of whom had no IT management experience. IT was far removed from the corporate leadership team and had no seat at the leadership table and no voice in strategic discussions. At best, IT was a fragmented, tactically focused afterthought—in short, a technical support group.

In the absence of standardization of PC equipment or communications infrastructure, professionals working in one location had difficulty communicating with professionals in other locations, and professionals traveling had difficulty communicating with people at their home base. At a time when companies were beginning to turn to personal-based IT solutions as enablers of efficiency and effectiveness, this fragmented IT situation was causing much tension within the leadership ranks and threatening to become a disabler of corporate growth and profitability.

The new CIO, a business executive and customer-focused professional who had been selected from within the company, knew that he had to act quickly to stabilize the IT organization, reconstruct the infrastructure, and begin enhancing the company's abilities to use technology to help drive revenue growth, cost reduction, and profitability.

The Turnaround Begins

The CIO knew that a large part of the IT turnaround effort would involve building strong relationships with all of his various constituencies. This meant communicating openly with everyone about the realities of IT and the IT organization, defending members of his organization against unreasonable requests and demands, managing the expectations of users—from professionals in the business unit to leaders in the executive suite, educating leaders at the corporate and business-unit level about what the enterprise was truly spending on IT and what the role of IT ought to be going forward, and beginning to break down a "feudal" system whereby local offices refused to share IT resources for the good of the company. On top of that, he had to dismantle power blocks in the IT organization and steer the various elements of the organization in the same direction—a job akin to herding cats.

To accomplish this, the CIO began to manage IT as if it were a business unit that *was* expected to function like a profit center. He also began maneuvering his way into the executive suite, taking every opportunity to meet individually with other C-level executives and regularly attending the leadership meetings. In addition, he:

- Assembled and installed a senior IT management team, consisting of executives with experience in marketing, human resources, operations, and finance. As the "CEO of the IT business unit," he began to legitimize IT in the eyes of business-unit and corporate leaders, to demonstrate that he could lead a high-performance team comprised of all the various advisors any CEO would need, and to gain visibility in the day-to-day workings of the IT organization that CIOs who focus exclusively on technology can never have.

- Established direct and open dialogue with the leaders of each business unit to understand their concerns and issues about IT.

- Instituted an open-door policy throughout the IT organization. Through an electronic bulletin board system, the CIO opened communication with IT staff at all levels, letting them know they could bring their concerns to him electronically, over the telephone, or face-to-face. He also directed his HR professional to begin work on a structured career model for IT staff that, for the first time, would establish clear career paths that could go in the direction of technology or of IT management.

Within two months, the CIO convened a meeting of IT leadership and many of the IT staff and used the meeting to reinforce the IT vision of enhancing the company's strategic goals, the IT organization's mission of providing the best quality of service to users to enable them to provide the best for their customers, and the IT organization's operating principles (dedication, honesty, and hard work).

Within six months, the CIO began issuing quarterly IT unit operating reports electronically and on paper to update the various constituencies about the IT unit's performance, performance improvements, and major projects.

These efforts energized the IT organization, and the business-unit leaders and users began to notice changes in attitude and in service level. The CIO served as a buffer between them and the day-to-day demands of corporate and business-unit technology users. He acted as a filter that let through only the best ideas from outside the IT organization and kept the IT staff focused on implementing those ideas by freeing them from distractions created by new user demands.

At the same time, the CIO began traveling to company locations around the country and the world to meet with IT staff members to get to know and understand their concerns. He also met with business-unit leaders and regional office management to help them understand the value of tying their IT efforts to those of other units around the world and to the corporate CIO's enterprisewide initiatives.

A major breakthrough occurred three months into his tenure when employees told him about a small group of individuals who were attempting to sabotage many of his efforts and were intimidating IT employees who were attempting to implement the new IT vision. The fact that employees felt they could come to him with an issue so deep in the human infrastructure of the organization was both heartening and scary. The incident turned out to be more threatening to corporate integrity than even he imagined, and the effort to remove the small group of rogue employees was difficult, required expert outside assistance, and caused many sleepless nights.

But when the disruptive employees were dismissed, when the majority of the IT organization who wanted to move forward felt they could do so without threats, and when they felt happy to come to work, a marked change occurred in the organization. The CIO had earned their complete trust. They were ready to do their part in taking the company forward.

One IT

In the second year of the CIO's tenure—the year he had mapped out for restructuring and streamlining the IT organization and IT delivery—the company's senior leadership put in place a plan to manage its far-flung operations in a more truly global manner. Key to accomplishing this plan was to develop a global CIO organization and IT infrastructure on which the company's thousands of employees could rely.

Efforts to streamline the U.S. IT organization, which had more than 50 locations, had already begun. But extending this effort globally was another matter. Having previously worked extensively outside the United States before taking on his new role, the CIO understood intuitively that both business executives and IT staff outside the United States would potentially have negative reactions to being asked to reorganize IT on an American model.

In addition, language, culture, local business practices, and varying degrees of IT maturity in each country in which the company operated would also have an effect on the effort to standardize and streamline IT operations.

At the same time, some of the IT hardware, software, infrastructure, and management best practices in these countries were better than those brought to the fore in the U.S. standardization effort; the question was often one of scalability.

The CIO had to rely on the relationship management skills he had developed during his years working abroad and on the relationships with corporate leaders he had built during his first year as CIO to develop a workable action plan and an appropriate global-local balance for the prospective IT end state.

While business leaders in all countries had agreed in principle to operate the company more globally, IT was the first operational organization slotted to become fully global—a truly unique accomplishment for a large corporation and a tribute to the CIO's global business acumen.

The CIO began the globalization effort by meeting privately with the company's board, which was composed of the heads of operations in countries where the company did the majority of its work. They were all very happy to be consulted and cooperated with the CIO in reaching an understanding of what infrastructure, applications, and outside services could be standardized globally and which IT functions would remain unique to their respective countries. Through this consultative process, the CIO built important working relationships with the country leaders. These helped immensely with implementation as country leaders removed roadblocks put in place by lower level management and by professionals wishing to continue working in "the old way."

The CIO also worked with IT staff to create a profile of the IT organization, functions, and tasks in each of the more than 40 countries in which the company operated. Because the profile survey had been created by a global group of IT professionals, there was little resistance to using it as a means of gaining insight into each country's IT operations.

Finally, the CIO met extensively with each major country's business leaders, key users, and local IT staff to explain the overall strategic vision and plan and to seek advice and counsel on how to make these work effectively in each of the local countries. These visits were crucial in developing credibility.

IT leaders from a number of countries began meeting as a global IT leadership team, sharing technology, management, and implementation successes. A global project team was established to design the key standardized applications. Project team members became champions of rational globalization—a well thought out, planned, and orderly approach to achieving the most effective balance of global-regional-local activity and ownership—and were able to explain the benefits to their colleagues and business leaders in their home countries and to lead the roll-out efforts locally.

The moral of this story is that the relationships that the CIO built with the leaders and members of all of IT's various constituencies became the cornerstone of the foundation of IT organizational success. In addition, the CIO considered teaching members of the global IT organization the value of building their own relationships—within the IT organization and across the company's business-unit, functional, and geographic borders—to be a major part of his role. He did this by example, working directly with as many members of the IT teams as possible and by adjusting metrics and compensation approaches to reward such behavior. He was successful because he adopted a win–win balanced approach (Figure 3.3).

This story does not tell all about the new CIO's efforts over the first two years; that narrative would fill several volumes. And every effort was not successful. In some cases where relationships were weaker, difficulties between IT and the business units were more pronounced. In countries outside the United States with strong business cultures or with individual leaders who possessed strong personalities, globalizing and standardizing even modest pieces of the IT infrastructure were difficult to accomplish.

As in any organization, over time, other senior executives successfully chipped away at pieces of the CIO organization's effectiveness through the political gamesmanship that always occurs when success in getting things done is mistaken for an attempt by the CIO to build a powerful political base.

But because the CIO had, early on, articulated the IT organization's vision of how it could become a driver of business value and provided the organization with a coherent mission and strong and consistent operating principles, he easily was able to establish working relationships that were

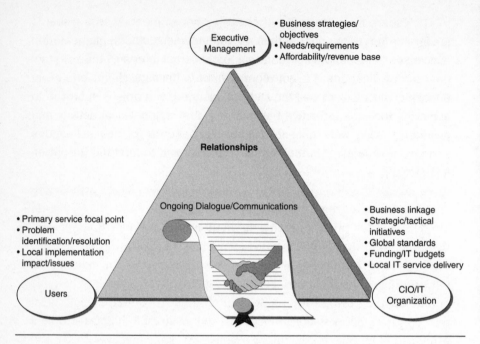

Figure 3.3   Win/Win Balanced Approach.

at least cordial with all of his peers among corporate and business unit leaders.

As important, the CIO imparted valuable lessons and skills to all members of the IT organization, helping them to play a part in moving IT forward as an integral component of the company. He made everyone in the IT organization an *enabler* of business value, dramatically multiplying and leveraging his effectiveness and his ability to deliver results and to communicate across the board.

CASE STUDY 3.3

The Value of Trusted Relationships

As part of a strategic corporate restructuring and divestiture program to split a major European-based manufacturing company into three distinct operating units, the global CIO had to separate the business processes and

IT infrastructure. Because the company's operations were spread around the world and relied on more than 40 separate systems, the business process and IT infrastructure separation would be complex.

The company began a large-scale project to manage all the activities required to effect the separation. This project involved teams composed of individuals from a number of different countries who rarely worked together. Midway through the process, a new CIO began his tenure.

Because of the large number of project participants and the complicated, often political dynamic that had developed, the new CIO began to question whether he, or anyone, had a clear understanding of the project status and key issues. In fact, he was seriously concerned that in the absence of effective IT leadership, intramural politics had already taken over. Ensuring effective management and an objective understanding of this high-profile project would be essential to its success.

The new CIO turned to a trusted outside advisor to create a planning workshop at which the major players in the project could gather and, through facilitated discussions, objectively assess where they were in the plan's time line and what problems were being encountered and possibly put aside inappropriately. The purpose of the workshop was also to create a more coherent plan for going forward. The CIO had previously worked with this advisor at another company, and they had established an excellent relationship. The CIO trusted the advisor's ability to deal with complex political IT situations.

A small team whose members possessed both business and technical knowledge interviewed lead project participants within the major work streams to establish an objective understanding of the project, its status, and its major risk factors. A workshop was convened that enabled participants to resolve some of their key concerns, keeping the focus on factual elements and critical success factors.

During the workshop, a number of very serious issues were raised that needed to be addressed. The project manager strongly believed that the outside advisor should not convey these issues directly to the CIO; he felt he could "work all these things out without escalating them and alarming anyone."

However, based on his relationship with the CIO, the advisor knew that he would want to be told firsthand about problems like this. He also knew that the CIO would handle the information discreetly. The advisor informed the project manager that he was going to talk to the CIO.

After the workshop, the outside expert presented a report to the CIO addressing project management, team dynamics, and areas of risk requiring more focus. As a result, the relationship carried the day, focused attention and action on the necessary issues, and helped achieve success.

In the absence of effective internal relationships based on trust and communication, executives often turn elsewhere to validate their feelings about issues with which they are uncomfortable. Because two executives are *internal* to the company does not always guarantee that they share a mutually trusting relationship.

All business executives want direct, objective, and candid input on important matters. Before making critical decisions, good executives want to speak with knowledgeable professionals whom they trust and from whom they can obtain a diversity of ideas.

If such relationships exist in a company, its executives typically go no further. However, if, for whatever reason, those relationships do not exist, effective executives seek professionals whose opinions they trust and value. A trusted individual, whether within the company or not, is always a most valued source of advice.

MANAGING OUTSOURCING RELATIONSHIPS

Another type of relationship that exists outside the company beyond the typical purchaser-vendor relationship is the outsourcing or partnering relationship. Whether to outsource all or part of a company's IT organization is one of the key decisions today's corporate executives make. Outsourcing can be a good way to accomplish either or both of two objectives:

1. It eliminates the need to upgrade both technology and IT skills by turning over the IT operations to a company that focuses strictly on provision of IT and, therefore, has both people and systems that are on the cutting edge of IT capabilities.
2. Outsourcing removes legacy systems from management's plate and enables the internal IT organization to focus on ramping up its people's technology skills to the cutting edge.

While outsourcing raises many issues about costs, metrics, and IT standardization, key concerns are the role of the corporate CIO in an organization where the provision of some or all IT services is outsourced and how the CIO manages the relationship with outsourcing providers.

To many CIOs and others in the IT organization, the O word—outsourcing—has multiple negative connotations. CIOs who embrace outsourcing usually do so at a tactical level. They view outsourcing as a way of ridding themselves of a series of discrete IT "problems" that have been thorns in their sides—items such as maintaining legacy systems, outfitting users with PCs, fixing broken equipment, answering help desk calls, and so on.

But there are other and better reasons to outsource. Figure 3.4 illustrates six reasons, ranging from the purely tactical (on the left) to the more strategic (on the right).

In most situations, people view agreements with outsourcing vendors as one-off, performance-based contracts through which they attempt to hold the vendors' feet to the fire. Although such agreements may reinforce the tactical, contractually based, metrics-driven, supplier-customer arrangement, they do not build trust-based, long-term, partnering relationships that are dedicated to the sharing and transfer of knowledge and experience and are focused on meeting the continuously changing goals of the company (and, therefore, of the IT organization).

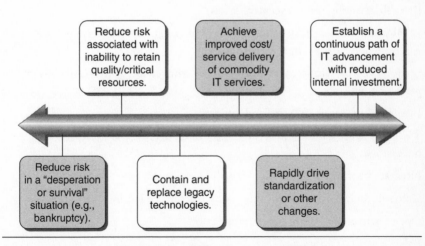

Figure 3.4   Why Outsource IT?

Establishing and building such partnering relationships with outside third parties require hard work on both sides. These relationships do not just happen because a contract has been signed. The most successful relationships with outside parties in the IT space occur because the CIO understands the difference between a business-partnering relationship deal and a deal oriented toward beating up the vendor.

In a partnering relationship, the outside vendor becomes an integral member of the CIO's team, and the IT organization has some skin in the game as well. Both sides are accountable for meeting performance measures. Such relationships build long-term confidence and trust, are focused on the company's goals and objectives, and create the win–win scenario that characterizes all partnering relationships.

A strictly contractual relationship sets the stage for endless finger pointing. The parties frequently use the contract and performance metrics as sticks with which to beat each other. The result is that both parties spend so much time focusing on how the other party has not lived up to the contractual language that neither spends much time focusing on the business objectives that the contract was designed to meet.

The CIO who acts as a business-unit leader organizes third parties into win-win relationships that maximize the potential to meet business

Table 3.2   Critical Success Factors: Outsourcing/Partnering

Key relationships at top executive levels.

Application of client relationship/account management/partnering concepts and principles (from a buyer's perspective).

Long-term win/win scenarios versus short-term vendor/contract, single-thread, price-only mentality.

Integrated processes (internal and external).

Total cost approach to ensure full impact of all decisions is explored and understood.

Integrated performance metrics across key processes.

Constant focus on improvements—costs and service levels.

Open environment with shared information.

Balance and flexibility.

objectives. This may or may not achieve the absolute lowest price per unit with respect to the outsourcing service being purchased. However, when one factors out the cost in people's time and aggravation resulting from the friction involved in a strictly contractual relationship, the true *life cycle cost* of the partnering-model outsourcing relationship may indeed be less.

Table 3.2 highlights some critical success factors for an outsourcing partnership model; Table 3.3 presents some key outsourcing/partnering principles.

Having participated in numerous outsourcing discussions, negotiations, and implementations, I saw one of the most successful arrangements when the corporate CIO of a company directly engaged the CEO of the out-sourcing company, and they created a personally agreed-on set of joint working principles for their respective teams to follow. Although these working principles were not legal contractual documents, the trust-based relationship they established and exhibited because of these principles set the tone from the top as to how they expected their teams to work together as one in the best interests of the company.

Table 3.3   IT Outsourcing/Partnering Principles

You cannot outsource your problems—especially IT leadership/management problems.

Fully understand your IT strengths, weaknesses, and cost base up front.

Whether you perform operational IT functions/activities in-house or outsource them, you will always need competent IT leadership/management capabilities.

When you outsource IT, you need an expanded IT management team with strong leadership and performance measurement capabilities to ensure that IT is run like a business.

Think carefully about which IT components to outsource (commodity functions) and which to retain (strategic/management/measurement functions).

Outsourcing is not a static end-state. It is a process (and journey) that evolves and changes over time and that is linked to and based on evolving business needs.

Ensure that outsourcing relationships and agreements have flexibility built in from the start so that you can make cost-effective adjustments with speed, while maintaining quality of service.

One of the most important and most misunderstood facts about out-sourcing is that it does not eliminate the need within the company for highly competent and capable IT leaders and managers. The nature of their jobs might have to change—from managing operations to managing provider relationships. But this change does not negate the need for communication, strategic planning, and project management skills. In fact, it makes such skills all the more important.

Added to these are those skills necessary to negotiate contracts that provide for long-term, flexible, mutually beneficial relationships along a

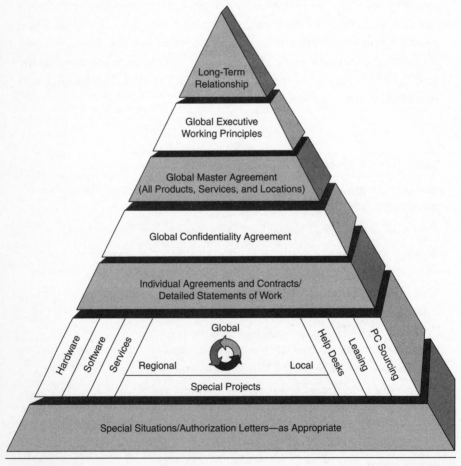

Figure 3.5   Overview/Hierarchy of Agreements, Contracts, and Services.

multitude of planes, including those related to the acquisition of hardware and software products, a variety of IT services, and the execution of special projects (Figure 3.5).

CASE STUDY 3.4

Establishing the Right Kinds of Outsourcing Arrangements

A provider of industry-specific information services wished to procure IT hardware, software, and services effectively and efficiently to help achieve its global strategy. Recognizing that IT work would outpace available resources, the CIO determined that a proper strategy and approach was needed for IT procurement, including outsourcing/partnering arrangements.

In moving forward with selective outsourcing/partnering arrangements, the CIO adopted a set of operating principles to ensure that the focus of these arrangements was on the long-term relationships necessary to establish and sustain the most appropriate total spend and service levels over time.

In addition, recognizing that some key IT hardware, software, and service providers were among the company's important customers, the CIO established processes whereby the IT organization could work closely with all relevant stakeholders inside the company, including those who sold the company's products and services to potential outsourcing partners. This would ensure that procurement decisions and activities would always be sensitive to these important relationships. The CIO used the critical success factors and key principles illustrated in Tables 3.2 and 3.3 as the basis for establishing relationships with outsourcing providers.

The CIO knew that different needs required different procurement sourcing/partnering arrangements. Therefore, he established three categories to describe the three general sets of needs:

1. *Strategic needs* had global impact, were considered by the CIO to be of global strategic importance, had a projected contract value of more than $500,000 annually, and, if not met, could have a negative impact on the company's business.
2. *Important needs* had a major national or regional impact or a less-than-major global impact and had a projected contract value of more than $100,000 annually.

3. *Tactical needs* were relatively short-term in nature, had only a local impact, and had a projected contract value of less than $100,000 annually.

The IT procurement mission was to guarantee the uninterrupted provision of IT hardware, software, and services to the company's personnel worldwide. Procurement activities were to be coordinated globally to ensure that the company had the best available technology and seamless support worldwide and to maximize the company's purchasing power with vendors.

The procurement/outsourcing/partnering process began with a vision of developing long-term relationships with key suppliers. Global executive working principles were developed jointly with key partners to guide the executive-level relationships that were built with key suppliers around the world. This established the pinnacle of the pyramid illustrated in Figure 3.5. Subsequently, global master agreements and global confidentiality agreements could be developed, followed by the portions of any agreement that covered the specific products or services being provided. Suppliers were required to embrace and implement open and direct communications with the company and to meet periodically with management.

Working principles included the following:

- Suppliers were to develop and maintain a relationship with management that was unique, flexible, and responsive to the company's requirements. Arrangements were to emphasize speed, superior execution, and effectiveness, while minimizing bureaucracy.
- The relationships between the company and its third-party partners were to be based and built on trust and mutual respect.
- Supplier employees and subcontractors were to be sensitized to the highest degree of confidentiality required by the confidentiality agreement. Both parties were to act in a similar manner and demonstrate sensitivity to the information and business practices of the other party.

Specific expectations were also developed to define the criteria for a *winning* global supplier:

- Measurably high-quality product or service
- Consistent global price

- Payment in a single currency, billed to a single address
- Local offices and high-quality account relationship personnel
- Consistent, 24/7 virtual support (phone, website, and e-mail)
- Preferred customer status
- Local and global summary reports of business transactions.

Service delivery and other metrics were to be defined, established, and monitored by joint company-supplier management teams. The suppliers' account relationship managers were to be strong communicators and relationship builders, while also being credentialed with appropriate technical, functional, or industry expertise. They also needed to be flexible and persistent in identifying and leveraging improvement opportunities.

Over time, the CIO established such relationships with only a handful of companies that could truly meet the challenge of being strategic partners with management in carrying out the company's endeavors.

WHAT THE CEO CAN DO TO ENSURE THAT THE CIO IS A MASTER OF RELATIONSHIP MANAGEMENT

Relationship management cannot be taught in a two-day course. It is learned primarily through apprenticeship as individuals work together over time in teams with people who do it well, understand the positive implications of doing it, and are willing to overtly model it for others.

CEOs can take five concrete steps to ensure that the company's CIO is a master of relationship management:

1. Make sure the CIO understands the importance of effective relationship management to his or her overall long-term success at the company and to his or her ability to be accepted as a peer by the other members of the executive management team.
2. Recognize that if the CIO has come up through the IT ranks, he or she might not have the type and level of relationship management skills needed to operate effectively as a business-unit leader on the executive management team.
3. Become a personal mentor to the CIO concerning relationship management, or ask a senior and trusted executive to fill the mentor role. Establish specific relationship management development/improvement

goals and work with the CIO over an extended period of time to hone his or her key relationship management skills.

4. Establish a seasoning process for the CIO similar to what a future business–unit CEO would go through. Put in place in the company a way for future IT leaders to get this seasoning before they rise to the level of CIO. Such a seasoning process includes working in different business units and in different geographic locations, rotating into key business–unit and/or corporate staff slots, and working for a time in a position close to the customer.

5. CEOs who are not comfortable either with their or a colleague's ability to assist the CIO in building strong relationship management skills should supplement their mentoring with outside professionals who will work directly with the CIO to develop these important capabilities.

CHAPTER 4

Align the IT Organization Structure with Profitability Drivers

Linking Technology to Business Objectives

A multinational manufacturer of industrial equipment was three years into an effort to standardize all systems in its equipment division by employing a common software platform. Although the company had already expended a significant amount of effort and cost, only one of eight plants was using the new standard system. The corporate CIO was concerned about the rate of progress in the division and asked an outside advisor for an opinion.

Working with the corporate CIO and the division's president, the outside advisor focused on one plant, a business unit that manufactured power tools used in cabinet manufacturing and other industries. In this plant, as in other operating units of the division, debate raged on among users, who claimed that the system was too complex, and IT, which claimed that users were not taking full advantage of the system.

The division's president, who had become personally involved in the dispute, ordered the CIO to find a solution that would enhance customer service and profitability and to do so quickly because the division was hemorrhaging.

Despite the new system in this business unit, inventory levels remained high and customer stock-outs were frequent. Over a 16-week period, an analysis of the business unit's inventory turns, customer order fill rates, purchasing lead times for key items, production lot sizes, and a host of other measures revealed that there was room for considerable improvement in operations.

A preliminary redesign of business processes at this plant suggested that manufacturing lead times could be reduced by approximately 50 percent without affecting the system. After examining the situation carefully, the president agreed to conduct a full pilot at the plant, and the results actually surpassed the 50 percent reduction effort.

The company recognized that focusing on the business issues resulted in significant benefits, including the ability to greatly simplify the requirements for its information systems. For example, the reduced lead times translated into less work-in-process inventory, which in turn simplified production tracking needs.

An alternative to the company's standard system was proposed, accepted, and implemented at a cost of 20 percent less than the initial estimate. The system was far simpler and thus received more user support. Because the simplified system was so effective in this plant, it replaced the more complex system being used in many other plants throughout the division and the company as a whole.

By more effectively linking business needs and focusing on business objectives rather than just on the technology, the company achieved significant breakthroughs in reducing lead times, inventories, and operating costs.

CEOs who expect IT to drive real results must curb their own desires and those of their business–unit leaders for *fad du jour* (FDJ) technology and IT projects. They need to ensure that IT priorities and resources are clearly aligned with other drivers of shareholder value. And they must make sure that IT does not suffer because of decisions made by others to institutionalize in complex systems inefficient and ineffective operating practices. They also need to ensure that IT is not funded at a level that makes it impossible to meet the demands of both corporate leadership and of users. Aligning the IT organization with the business's key profitability drivers is fundamental to optimizing business value from IT.

In its January 2003 strategic analysis report, "Running IS Like a Business: Introducing the ISCo Model," Gartner crystallizes the conflict that arises when corporations look on their IT/IS organization as a support cost center rather than as an internal services company (ISCo):

> The most worrisome of these relationships are with the consumers and business managers, because their interests often conflict. Business managers typically fund the internal provider through a fixed budget, overhead allocation, direct chargeback or some combination of the three. They are most interested in balancing the benefits of service with its costs, and often determine that a less-than-perfect service experience is acceptable at a given level of funding; for example that receiving incrementally better service is not worth the price. The services are funded at "good enough" levels. Unfortunately, they (business leaders) rarely communicate this rational to their organizations. As a result, consumers of a service— for the IS organization, the end users—expect service perfection. They do not understand the performance constraints placed on the service provider by virtue of business leader funding decisions. They become dissatisfied, then express that dissatisfaction to their leaders, who fail to make the connection between funding constraints and performance constraints. They (end users) develop the perception that the internal provider is delivering low value, which creates increased outsourcing pressures.[1]

The ISCo model proposed by Gartner helps to remove some of the biggest barriers IT organizations face in providing top-quality services to their users. These include the view that IT services are "free" to users, the notion that the IT organization has unlimited capacity, the myth that the demand for these IT services can be infinite, and, finally, the misperception that the delivery of IT services will always be perfect. Gartner's ISCo model places real-world value (from a P&L perspective) on IT, with the value being defined by the buyer of the services. This forces users to consider IT, as they would any other business unit entity, as being akin to a capital market, that is, driven by supply, demand, and pricing.

However, companies do not have to move their IT organizations all the way to the ISCo model (with its implicit issues of internal transfer pricing)

---

[1] Colleen Young, Gartner (January 16, 2003).

to run them like businesses. The issue is not about imposing a formal P&L structure on the IT organization. It is about developing IT leaders who can join with other corporate leaders to create a fully integrated business strategy that uses IT appropriately and run the IT organization in a businesslike manner, with appropriate professional disciplines in place.

Prerequisites for an IT organization that focuses on business issues and helps drive shareholder value are:

1. A CIO who understands and *lives* the business, not just the technology
2. A flexible, networked, and even virtual IT organization team structure
3. An agile, capable, adaptable, change-embracing IT workforce.

A CIO WHO UNDERSTANDS AND LIVES THE BUSINESS

For the IT organization to organize its efforts around drivers of business value, the CIO must understand what those drivers are, how to recognize them and parse them, and what effects IT can have on them. For the CIO, that means living rather than just observing the business.

The CIO and top IT managers need to be able to listen to business-unit leaders describing what they would like from technology and then to say, "No, that is not what you need, because that will not really have an impact on your business's drivers." In addition, they need to have enough credibility so that when they say no, the business-unit leader accepts that answer as a professional decision and not as a personal affront.

For example, in the 1990s, two large information services companies merged. One company's IT organization was centralized and under the direction of a global CIO; the other company's IT organization was decentralized. The CIO and another senior leader in his company debated about the extent to which the company's move to a new technology infrastructure could be continued during the merger process and about the extent to which those efforts would have to be put on hold while the IT systems of the two companies were integrated.

Because the CIO believed that the new technology really did not affect business efficiency or effectiveness, he argued that the company's primary goal was to make sure that the legacy companies' e-mail systems worked together on Day One. He felt that it was essential for people throughout the merged company to be able easily and rapidly to communicate and share information. He argued that within six months to a year, a new, uniform desktop suite would have been implemented across the merged enterprise and, at that point, his organization could get back to working on the new technology infrastructure without interfering with the legacy companies' integration efforts. Because the CIO understood both the business and IT needs, especially those related to integrating the communications throughout the merged company, he was able to hold the line and ensure that only the most crucial Day One IT priorities were addressed.

Drivers of Shareholder Value

Major drivers of shareholder value include:

- Revenue and earnings growth
- Capital spending
- New distribution channels
- Cash flow management/financial engineering
- Cost reduction
- R&D/innovation
- Marketing/advertising.

The relative importance of these drivers is determined by changes in the economy, the industry in which the business operates, and/or the business itself, or even by a change in the company's CEO. Technology and information systems must be robust enough to markedly support these drivers, yet flexible and agile enough to accommodate changes that impact them.

Revenue and Earnings Growth.   Revenue growth can be organic or driven by acquisitions. Organic growth is slower, and the pace of transition from the current state to the growth objective is slower than growth by acquisition. With organic growth, IT systems and use of IT can be evolutionary rather than revolutionary; IT needs to focus on systems that can do "more of the same." Scalability is key. Growth through acquisition causes spikes, bumps, and large, discrete incremental increases in the number of transactions that need to be processed. In addition, acquisitions bring in totally new businesses and, with them, new business drivers.

Bringing new IT hardware, software, and people into an IT organization creates integration risks, a need for IT due diligence skills to determine which systems can be meshed and which need to be brought over from one system to the other (the acquired company may have better technology), huge volume increases at a single point in time, and system architecture and service level issues.

Even companies growing organically can experience an IT crisis such as the one illustrated in Case Study 4.2.

CASE STUDY 4.2

Managing Risk to Prevent Disaster

A multilevel producer and distributor of consumer products had undergone a disastrous implementation of a new distribution system and lost control of its entire North American inventory. The company had always lagged behind others of its size and scale in terms of IT; its IT organization was very fragmented and immature; and it did not know its true IT costs or priorities.

A third-party contractor managed much of the distribution system implementation with little oversight from the CIO who, as it turned out, was looking for a new job at the time. When the CIO departed, the company's lack of IT management processes and oversight by senior business leaders or capable second-tier IT professionals left the organization in disarray. The IT group was simply not organized effectively to handle the business's needs.

The company's recently appointed CEO asked a seasoned non-IT executive to take over as CIO. Quickly recognizing that the IT organization was in chaos and that the failed distribution system implementation threatened the entire company, he called on outside experts to help him assess the overall situation, determine the immediate crisis-management actions that needed to be taken, and stabilize the order-management and distribution system.

While a team worked with IT staff on the latter objective, another team worked with the CIO to assess the overall IT organization, its key management resources and processes, and the company's total IT spend and to develop a governance model for future IT activities and expenditures. The results of this effort helped the CEO and the company's board more effectively understand the significant impact that IT currently had and would continue to have on the business. This in turn led them to place increasing emphasis on monitoring IT expenditures and on making sure they met business goals.

The company, the CEO, and the board simply could not afford the embarrassment and economic impact of another failure of this proportion. They were focused in a laserlike fashion on managing their IT business risk going forward.

Capital Spending.   Capital spending is defined as using capital to acquire new plants and equipment, thereby generating internal growth or renewal. IT can be used to enhance capital spending in a number of ways. By using information technology instead of capital, in the form of people or machinery, a company can maximize its capital spending by achieving various types of productivity improvements and economies of scale. IT can reduce head count in ways that range from using robotic manufacturing to self-diagnosis of machinery and reduction of maintenance personnel.

One company in the food distribution industry did a very effective job of using IT capital investment to reduce the head count at its primary mixing and distribution centers. By installing state-of-the-art warehouse management and automated storage and picking systems, they reduced the labor required at each location by 60 percent. Because of the significantly enhanced speed and accuracy of the new system, these near-lights-out facilities were able to reduce inventory storage requirements and increase inventory turns by a factor of three.

New Distribution Channels.   With new distribution channels, a company can reach new customers in new markets. E-business is possibly the largest new distribution channel that has ever become available. However, when any new distribution channel is opened, channel conflicts and cannibalization inevitably occur. As many are finding over time, e-business's biggest boon may be as an efficiency tool to help businesses reach their more traditional distribution channels, including distributors, jobbers, and retailers.

Media is one area in which technology completely changed the method of distribution. For example, the Internet has enabled software developers to distribute their products digitally and producers of recorded music and film to enable customers to download their offerings on a pay-per-use or purchase model.

CASE STUDY 4.3

Digital Distribution Transforms an Industry

Five companies account for 75 percent of worldwide revenues in the recorded music industry. These companies have been moving toward digital distribution since the late 1990s as a way to combat economic and competitive pressures brought on by computer and video game manufacturers and ever more fragmented and localized music tastes.

In the traditional recorded music model, artists enter into a contract with a recording label to produce a fixed number of albums, CDs, and/or tapes. Labels handle production, marketing, and distribution and generate revenue through product sales as well as through royalties. Retailers extend the artist-label relationship to the consumer.

As Robin D. Gross points out, "The continual expansion of bandwidth capabilities through the use of fiber optic cable and satellite technologies clears the path for near immediate transmissions of large files over the Web. At current Internet download speeds, a typical three-minute, thirty-second song in the common MP3 format takes 3.7 minutes to download over an ISDN line, 18 seconds over a T1, and only 3 seconds using a cable modem. Teledesic Network, a 288 global satellite system currently in development called 'Internet in the Sky' promises to deliver the same song for less than half a second from the first day of the network's service. In terms of the digital distribution of entertainment, songs, music videos, graphics, and advertisements, the possibilities seem endless."[2]

Although most of the recorded music industry viewed digital distribution as a threat (e.g., consumers downloading free music to their hard drives or MP3 players), an IT analysis performed for one company revealed how it could use technology to leapfrog distributors and cut costs by developing Internet distribution channels. It also demonstrated how the company could capitalize on market changes by focusing not on its established reputation but on speed and new alliances with other media channels, such as film, video, and television, thereby leveraging complementary products. Although the story is far from over in the entertainment and media industry and all

---

[2] "The Digital Music Revolution" (November 1998). Available at www.virtualrecordings.com /digital_music.htm.

of the major competitors are using these new technologies, digital distribution has dramatically and forever changed the dynamics, economics, and overall industry business model.

_____

Cash Flow.   Cash flow drives business performance by accelerating income and decelerating outflow to the company's benefit. Using information technology to reduce the level of inventory that must be carried improves cash flow because cash is not tied up in inventory. Decision support, treasury management, cash collection systems, when brought to the fore, are examples of how a company can use technology to improve cash flow.

CASE STUDY 4.4

Outsourcing Can Mean Survival

A major company involved in engineering services was in the middle of a strategic business survival crisis, looking for all possible cost reduction opportunities to help restore cash flow and remain solvent. Creditors were pushing the company closer and closer to bankruptcy proceedings to salvage what they could.

This decades-old company prided itself on being a pioneer in engineering and in developing new technologies for use within the telecommunications industry. IT was core to the business's strategy, but it was addressed mainly from a technical and engineering perspective rather than as a management lever. The company had done a poor job of reshaping itself as new technologies began to make obsolete many of its core products and services. As the company began to fall on difficult times, it failed to respond quickly enough to market forces.

As revenues dropped and layoffs began, the board forced the CEO to resign and brought in a new CEO to reenergize and restructure the company. The new CEO engaged a number of outside advisors in a last-ditch effort to reduce costs radically throughout the company and to free up enough cash to enable the business to survive long enough to attempt a turnaround. The IT advisors were specifically asked to assess the current situation in the IT organization and to identify immediate actions that could be taken to free up significant amounts of cash. At the same time, they were asked to develop a plan that would protect the operating integrity of the network and take into account the centrality of IT to the company's strategy and the numerous IT R&D projects that were underway.

The advisors began their work by performing a highly focused IT spend analysis, finding areas of low and high costs. They began to analyze the data in an orderly fashion, looking for opportunities to reduce costs. However, it soon became apparent that the company's financial condition was deteriorating on a daily basis. Highly experienced IT people, fearing the worst, were leaving the company in droves for other jobs.

Though dramatic cuts in IT spending were necessary to help alleviate the company's cash crisis, it was also necessary to stop the exodus of skilled IT personnel required to run the company's network.

The IT advisors determined that the only way to accomplish both of these objectives was to approach a premier outsourcing provider for the purpose of executing an outsourcing and financing deal within 90 days and to turn the company's entire IT infrastructure and skills base over to the outsourcer to ensure a stable operating IT platform for the company and its customers. The outsourcing company would also be asked to accept an unorthodox form of payment for its services that was not consistent with current practice or with its standard mode of operation.

Whereas traditional, conservative behavior would have mandated a full-scale bidding proposal and evaluation process involving multiple vendors, time constraints, and the risk of a complete financial meltdown dictated a nontraditional approach.

The integrity of the outside consultant's spend analysis was an important element in getting both the company and the outsourcer to agree to a unique arrangement. *The outsourcer was willing to accept an independent analysis of the IT spend, rather than conduct its own six-month assessment, and close the outsourcing deal within a 90-day period.* The company was able to free up significant amounts of cash through the outsourcing arrangement and survive, albeit as an extremely streamlined entity.

Cost Reduction.   Executives who see IT only as a cost that should be reduced are short-term thinkers. Leaders who look to the longer term see IT as a strategic lever that can be used to effect cost cutting in other areas of the company.

Some companies view cost savings as a cyclical "fatten up, slim down" exercise that is performed during market downturns to offset lack of growth and lost revenue. However, such an approach works neither in personal weight control nor in running a business effectively.

In the corporate world, one of the dangers of cyclical cost cutting is that it forces the view that IT spending is an indulgence that can be excised from the corporate diet during lean times. In the IT organization, this view results in a roller-coaster-like series of ups and downs that affects not only technology investment, but also service delivery. It also impacts IT's ability to link tightly with business strategy and to retain top-performing talent.

Other companies view cost savings as a continuous activity. They constantly strive to achieve economies and savings, and they regularly invest in technology (even in difficult times) to drive efficiencies and reduce costs. These companies have mastered the idea of technology as a business enabler. They understand the correlation between IT effectiveness and wise IT spending that drives more efficient and effective business processes.

The IT organization in such a company is a part of the ongoing cost savings effort, and because the CIO operates it as a real business unit, he or she is held to the same cost savings standards as other business-unit leaders. For these companies, the IT organization is completely in synch with the company's profitability drivers.

In lean times, these CIOs weather the storm along with the entire company and know exactly where, when, and how to tighten the IT belt. Successful IT organizations that operate in this manner are not victims of corporate directives. Rather, they are fully contributing business-unit partners.

The CEO of a company I worked with over a period of time was lamenting the fact that his IT organization never seemed to finish anything it started. He asked me to see if I could determine what the problem was. One of the first things I noticed when I examined the IT budgets for the past several years was a classic pattern of providing funding in one year and removing funding in the next. Many IT efforts in the company had been launched, but because they often spanned more than one fiscal year, most were never completed because costs were cut and funding was rescinded. This created a continuous up and down cycle for IT and much wasted spending. IT was viewed as a cost that could be turned on and off like a faucet, regardless of the downstream impact of the ups and downs of the spend.

R&D/Innovation.   Not all companies in all industries depend on R&D and innovation as primary levers to drive earnings, profitability, and shareholder value. But in industries where R&D and innovation are important, technology often plays one of three important roles:

1. In some cases, the technology is simply used as a tool to enhance, streamline, or facilitate the R&D process. An example is an automated R&D tracking and compliance system that a company in the pharmaceutical industry might use to help manage its portfolio of R&D projects and spend.
2. In other cases, the technology is the main foundation or platform on which the R&D or innovation takes place, for example, early e-business/e-commerce platforms that had the effect of changing the retail business model.
3. Finally, cases exist where technology *is* the R&D and innovation, for example, the digitization and electronic distribution of content in the recorded music industry discussed earlier.

An overview of these three scenarios is provided in Figure 4.1.

In each of these scenarios, IT plays a different role. The further across the continuum (from support to main business component) a company moves, the more integral IT becomes to the business and, therefore, the greater its role and influence in the strategic business planning process.

In addition, as a company moves further across the continuum, its IT organization must become more robust, well developed, and professionally managed. However, this does not in any way suggest that a company that finds itself at the left end of the continuum should not manage its IT as a business. The company should, but the intensity and volume of formal processes and measurements may be different.

A company I assisted had made numerous acquisitions over a five-year period, resulting in diversified holdings in three distinct industries—food products, retailing, and online information services. These were three very different industries, each requiring a very different approach toward IT R&D spending. The food products group needed to use basic standard

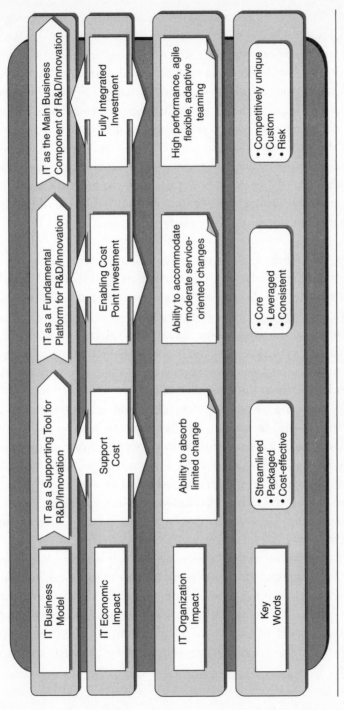

Figure 4.1 R&D and Innovation IT Impact Continuum.

IT capability reasonably well and did not need to be on the leading edge. The retailing group needed to do the same but also to focus some IT R&D investment money on certain specialized retail applications and technologies that could add a level of strategic competitive advantage. The online information services group needed to be at the forefront of IT R&D investment, developing and using leading edge technologies to enable the business to compete effectively in the digital environment. This R&D map, when overlaid onto the R&D and innovation technology impact continuum, was actually spread across multiple segments. However, by being specific and granular about IT R&D expenditures based on the different needs of each industry group, the company was able to do an effective job of spending its IT R&D investment money more wisely.

Marketing/Advertising.   To varying degrees, companies rely on marketing and advertising to enhance their overall market position and drive earnings, profitability, and shareholder value. The extent to which technology and the IT organization enable this process varies as well.

Obtaining and analyzing large volumes of customer-related data (e.g., demographics, buying patterns, trend information) are longstanding business practices. Technology has certainly made the collection and analysis process easier, quicker, and more cost effective.

Large back-end processing capability and good front-end, user-friendly analysis and reporting tools have long been the workhorses that help businesses in their marketing efforts. Some companies specialize in this work and sell their data sets and analysis services to others. The IT capability needed to support such efforts has tended to be organized, structured, and operated in a traditional, hierarchical manner to accommodate the predictable processing of large volumes of relatively homogeneous data.

The Internet altered that model in a number of ways. It enabled access to various combinations and permutations of customer-related data and information, making them exponentially richer than ever before. With the volume of data increasing, traditional back-end processing needs remained an important part of the IT equation, but the need for front-end, Web-based data collection, transport, and analysis tools dramatically increased.

A proliferation of such tools and configurations changed how the IT organization needed to be organized to address the constantly changing environment that was about to become the norm. Thus, the ability of the IT organization to add value to the business with respect to marketing and advertising has become increasingly dependent on its agility, flexibility, and adaptability to rapid and continuous change.

In the previous example related to IT R&D, some of the expenditures in both the retail group and the online information services group clearly helped make the marketing and advertising more effective.

A FLEXIBLE, NETWORKED, VIRTUAL, AND TEAM-BASED ORGANIZATION

Today's successful IT organization cannot be hierarchical. It must be fluid, team based, and driven by roles and skills. Problems must be "swarmed," and project or crisis teams often must be assembled on a just-in-time, ad hoc basis to ensure that the right skills are in place to deliver service on time, on budget, and to the right user constituency.

In some people's minds, hierarchical structure equates to management discipline, control, or accountability. This is not necessarily so. Corporate CEOs need to understand that IT is not analogous to accounts payable; it is not a static, routine, transaction-driven "support function." Rather, it is a dynamic entity that requires a constantly changing set of skills and flexibility in management to drive performance and to enhance corporate profitability.

The right IT skills from around the world, when shaped into high performance virtual teams, can double or triple an IT organization's effectiveness, productivity, speed, and quality of service delivery.

The key to improving customer satisfaction and management accountability is developing an organization that is focused, flexible, and agile. One example of the teaming approach to managing an IT organization is called "Plan, Build, Run" and is illustrated in Figure 4.2.

In the Plan, Build, Run structure, roles, responsibilities, and priorities for each group and each individual are clarified. Individuals assigned to *run* roles focus on customer service. Those assigned to *build* roles are project-driven. Those who have *plan* roles look at the big picture.

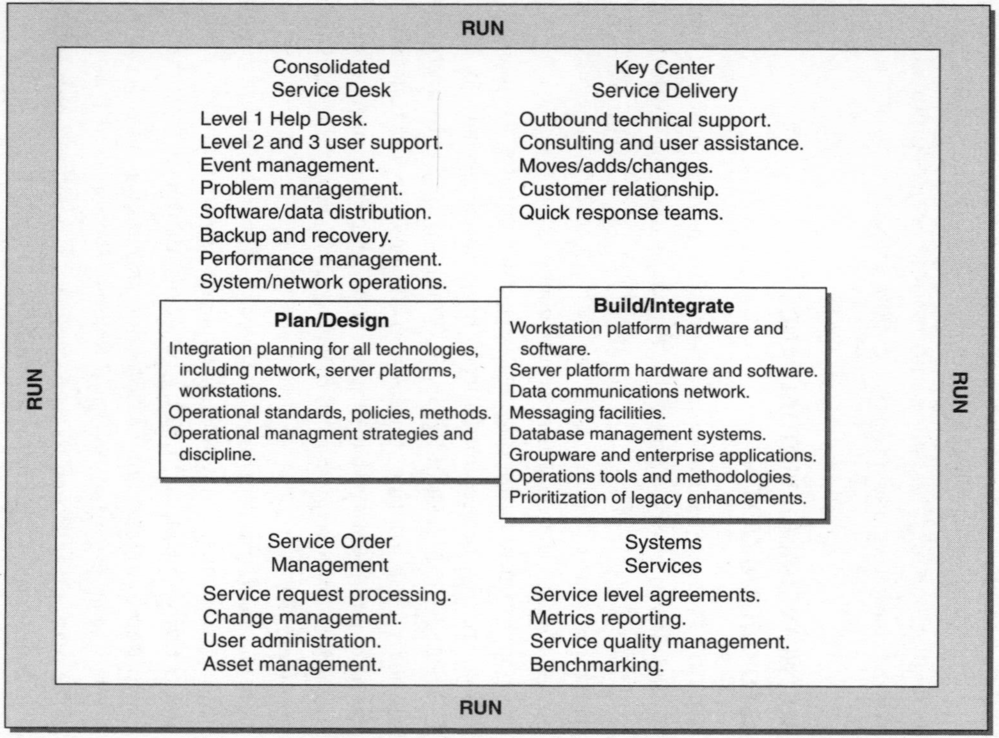

RUN

Consolidated
Service Desk

Level 1 Help Desk.
Level 2 and 3 user support.
Event management.
Problem management.
Software/data distribution.
Backup and recovery.
Performance management.
System/network operations.

Key Center
Service Delivery

Outbound technical support.
Consulting and user assistance.
Moves/adds/changes.
Customer relationship.
Quick response teams.

Plan/Design

Integration planning for all technologies,
including network, server platforms,
workstations.
Operational standards, policies, methods.
Operational managment strategies and
discipline.

Build/Integrate

Workstation platform hardware and
software.
Server platform hardware and software.
Data communications network.
Messaging facilities.
Database management systems.
Groupware and enterprise applications.
Operations tools and methodologies.
Prioritization of legacy enhancements.

Service Order
Management

Service request processing.
Change management.
User administration.
Asset management.

Systems
Services

Service level agreements.
Metrics reporting.
Service quality management.
Benchmarking.

RUN

Figure 4.2   The *Plan, Build, Run* IT Service Organization.

Within the build set of tasks and assignments, clear accountability exists for each component of the infrastructure. This model lends itself to an organizational matrix approach that requires moving staff through the IT organization through rotational assignments across technical disciplines and functional roles.

As technology has become more complex, IT staff members have become more specialized. But, from a customer (user) perspective, the technology is only an enabler of a business process. Users demand seamless delivery of increased availability, performance, and functionality.

The Plan, Build, Run model facilitates such delivery because it breaks down the barriers between traditional "silos" in an IT organization. Using the model enables more seamless integration of projects, service, and support activities and the resources necessary to carry them out. It also makes it easier for staff to move throughout the IT organization matrix through rotational assignments across multiple functional and technical disciplines.

CASE STUDY 4.5
Building a Global Team

The CIO of a global financial services company was asked to reorganize the IT function, which consisted of a collection of national and regional IT groups, into one global organization. An outside facilitator was asked to arrange a meeting of senior IT personnel from the various countries and regions, as well as of top IT people from the company's different functional units. IT teams had been working as isolated local groups. The meeting was intended to jump-start the process of global teamwork, enabling IT leaders to think about issues that affected the company around the world, to share best practices and successes, and to determine if these were replicable in other regions or countries.

The global IT group immediately turned its attention to implementing an upgraded global communication system throughout the company as an enabling technology that would help operating units work in a more global fashion. Team members nominated individuals from their local or regional organizations to work on a global, high-performance team that was given the task of designing and implementing this critical piece of the business's technology.

As it turned out, both the best local technology to build out as the global communications platform and the best manager to take on the project were located in Asia. The CIO, an American, felt this was wonderful because it would further embed the concept that both the IT organization and the company were truly global and not just trying to be American across the globe.

The project combined the knowledge gained by the Asian project manager during the implementation of his regional communications technology and the expertise of local IT staff from countries around the world. The team spent two months together working exclusively on this project, which was successfully implemented.

The ability to rapidly assemble the right team to design and roll out the new system globally in such a short time frame was really made possible by the working relationships and the trust that had been forged by the CIO with key country business and IT leaders over the prior months. The relationships, trust, and credibility established over time were the foundation for demonstrating how the global IT organization could work together to deliver globally oriented solutions that actually worked in local environments.

AN AGILE, CAPABLE, ADAPTABLE, AND CHANGE-EMBRACING WORKFORCE

Individuals in the IT organization need to understand the variety of roles they may be asked to play in providing services to various constituents. They need to be compensated based on their current and future roles and skills, their relative value in the marketplace, and their specific individual and team performance.

Key to building and maintaining an IT organization based on a high performance, high-quality team structure is reshaping what IT people do every day. The focus must be on transforming the IT organization from an aggregation of technical jobs involving discrete tasks and activities into a team of people seeking long-term professional careers. Such careers require well-planned skills evolution, development, and growth in the traditional technical areas. But growth and development in the *softer* nontechnical areas are as, or even more, important.

An IT organization that has established a proper career-model approach to managing and developing its professional staff will provide for a skills-based career development program designed to move the IT organization wherever it needs to go to ensure that it is fully aligned with and linked to the business's strategy and objectives.

A career model is what truly differentiates an IT organization and enables it consistently and quickly to reshape and realign itself with constantly shifting business objectives and with the profitability drivers associated with those objectives. This is the manner in which high performance business units of leading-edge companies organize themselves.

Establishing such an IT organizational model involves determining the right balance of functional, managerial, and geographic accountability and responsibility. It also involves understanding the specific skills and competencies required for each type of role necessary in the IT organization at any point in time. The career model puts flesh and blood on the concept of *managing IT as a business*. It also creates a strong and sustainable foundation for absorbing and adapting to continuous change.

The career model is a skills-based career development program. It is essentially a matrix containing activities and tasks that individuals working at various professional levels in the IT organization are expected to perform. Only after an individual has performed the requisite number of activities and tasks in each of the technical and business categories can he or she move to the next level on the professional growth matrix.

Several companies that I have worked with that have implemented some form of an IT career model have dramatically reduced their IT staff turnover and significantly enhanced their ability to grow their own staff internally particularly with regard to new IT skills. This, in turn, has had a substantial impact on holding the line and, in some cases, on reducing aggregate IT HR costs.

A blank career model matrix containing the technical and business activities and tasks that need to be performed is illustrated in Table 4.1.

Figure 4.3 illustrates the key components in the career model process, including those that each member of the IT organization must use when establishing his or her personal goals and objectives for the coming year and against which the IT staff member is measured and those for which IT management is responsible.

Table 4.1 Career Model Matrix

Key Competency Areas	Competency Levels				
	Level I	*Level II*	*Level III*	*Level IV*	*Level V*
Technical					
Operations and support.					
Deployment.					
Development and maintenance.					
Research and strategy.					
Business processes.					
Project management.					
Business-specific technical competencies.					
Industry-specific technical competencies.					
Business					
Using technology.					
Focusing customer needs.					
Developing talent.					
Managing teams.					
Developing and sharing personal knowledge.					
Working and communicating with others.					
Innovation.					
Business-specific business competencies.					
Industry-specific business competencies.					
Other					
As appropriate.					

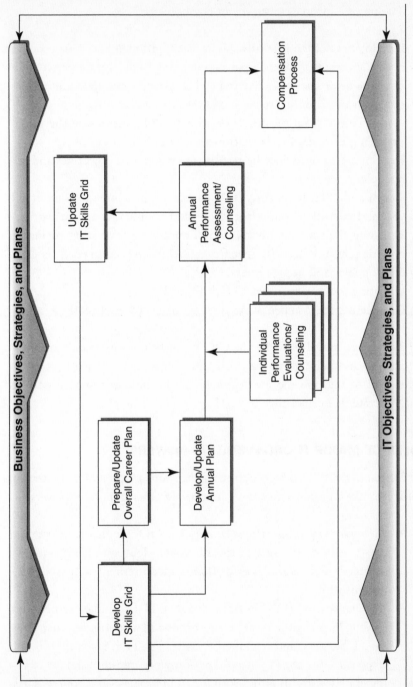

Figure 4.3   IT Career Model Overview.

The process involves seven major components:

1. Development of the IT skills grid by each staff member. This provides both a snapshot of where a person currently is and a prospective view of where he or she would like to be. The overall career plan and the annual plan are then used to fill in the specifics on how the individual intends to move from the current to the desired positions on the grid.
2. Preparing or updating the staff member's overall career plan.
3. Developing or updating the staff member's annual objectives and annual plan.
4. Conducting and preparing performance evaluations throughout the year and providing counseling to the staff member, as appropriate.
5. Assessing the staff member's overall annual performance, including providing him or her with specific counseling and action plans for skills development and improvement.
6. Updating the staff member's IT skills grid.
7. Completing the compensation review process for each staff member.

The career model provides the CIO with the tools necessary to inventory, assess, and build all of the skills and competencies of the IT organization and to manage more effectively the IT human resource pool to achieve strategic business needs.

ROLES OF MAJOR IT ORGANIZATION PLAYERS

In addition to the CIO, a high-performance, team-oriented IT organization that is run like a business includes a number of other important players:

- *IT organization operations chief* (IT-COO), in charge of ongoing day-to-day operations of the IT assets, delivery of high-quality services, and overall performance measurement across the IT organization.
- *IT finance chief* (IT-CFO), in charge of IT fiscal management, including building the business case around IT investments, managing the IT budgets, and tracking IT assets. The IT finance chief is also responsible for key IT financial performance measures and for working closely with his or her corporate and business-unit counterparts.

- *IT organization human resources director* (IT-HRD), in charge of managing the IT organization's human resource assets, leading the development and maintenance of the organization's career model, and working closely with HR counterparts throughout the company.
- *IT marketing/communications director* (IT-MCD), who works with the CIO and the entire IT organization to craft the appropriate messages for the various IT organization constituencies—from users to executive leaders—and to deliver those messages through the appropriate media at the right time. This individual is also responsible for assisting the entire IT organization to effectively communicate key information during major implementation, rollout, and IT crisis situations.
- *IT functional/technical leaders* (IT-F/TL), who are directly responsible for groups of people applying their specific IT functional and technical skills (e.g., telecommunications, network management, hardware, software) to the delivery of quality service throughout the company.
- *IT project managers* (IT-PM), who manage the various projects put in place to help IT create leverage and drive corporate profitability.
- *IT business-unit account managers* (IT-BUAM), who manage day-to-day relationships between the IT organization and the many business units and corporate functions that depend on the IT organization to provide them with enabling tools.

Of these, perhaps most important are the business-unit account managers (sometimes called *business-technology liaisons*).

Addressing customer service (business unit or corporate function) needs in a company with multiple operating business units and global operations requires the dedicated time of a group of account managers. These account managers perform the same tasks as an account manager from a service provider, including:

- Understanding the IT needs of the business unit
- Explaining cost and service level tradeoffs to the customer
- Acting as the go-to person for the customer if there are problems
- Facilitating the resolution of business-unit problems with IT people and IT problems with business-unit people

- Maintaining a balanced perspective and reducing emotional reaction among IT or business-unit staff during high-stress problem/crisis situations and keeping everyone focused on the primary objectives and critical tasks at hand.

Such individuals should have a distinct combination of training, experience, natural ability, and personality.

In this role, the account manager/liaison is constantly communicating priorities, needs, and desires from the business unit or corporate function to the IT organization and communicating the realities of the IT organization to the business unit or corporate function.

The account manager assists the one or two business units he or she works with in conducting strategic and tactical technology planning and works with members of the IT organization to help them understand how best to incorporate these plans into the overall IT planning work. He or she shares knowledge and best practices in unit technology planning with other members of the account management team.

From within the IT organization, the account manager communicates IT policies and procedures to the business unit or corporate function and the importance of standardization of hardware platforms, network infrastructure, and application software across the corporation. He or she also identifies and counsels about opportunities to leverage technology among business units or corporate functions, and, most importantly, communicates the status of IT organization initiatives and ongoing IT operations.

Finally, the account manager acts as a *single point of contact* for leaders and IT professionals in the customer business unit or corporate function if they encounter problems with IT, want clarification of service level agreements, or experience a sudden change in business climate that may require increases or decreases in IT services.

A large multinational industrial products company that set up its IT organization along the lines previously described was able dramatically to focus, clarify, and shift the perception of its primary users toward its overall professionalism. This was evidenced by a comparison of the results of a broad IT user survey conducted semiannually by the company. Comments provided in the survey indicated that within a period of six months after this type of organizational structure had been implemented, the users' overall perceptions of the IT organization were more professional because "they functioned much more like a real business unit, which caused us to trust them more."

HOW CAN INFORMATION TECHNOLOGY DESTROY SHAREHOLDER VALUE?

An inappropriate or poorly functioning IT organization can harm a company's operations and, in fact, destroy shareholder value in a number of ways, including:

- Execution failures
- Strategic failures
- Massive infrastructure failures
- Security failures.

Execution Failures

Generally, an execution failure is the inability to deliver satisfactorily the expected result or outcome concerning, for example, a project or a service metric. The result of an execution failure can range from poor customer service to a devastating business interruption.

The nature of the failure and the industry in which the business operates will dictate the severity of the business interruption and the downstream potential impact on shareholder value.

For example, in a company with a heavy daily transaction processing volume, a blow-up during conversion of the company's primary order-entry and distribution system would result in an inability to take orders and ship products. If this lasted for several days, customers would immediately find alternate sources of product; once customers leave, they may not come back.

If this happened once, the company would attempt a customer recovery program to get its customers back. However, if such a problem is chronic, the company's reputation will become tarnished, customers will lack confidence in the company and leave for good, and the impact on shareholder value will likely be substantial and sustained.

CASE STUDY 4.6

Using Technology to Manage Customer Relationships

One company developed, licensed, and supported application software designed to meet the needs of a specific industry's vertical market. Customers typically paid a one-time licensing fee to obtain the software and then paid an annual fee to access ongoing telephone support.

Rapid growth challenged the company's ability to provide adequate levels of customer service. Although sales (licensing) of the company's software had grown considerably over the previous five-to-seven years, customer complaints about telephone support were growing even faster. In some cases, the company was losing out on potential sales opportunities to competitors after prospects heard from references about difficulties reaching the company's telephone support staff.

As a result, the CIO persuaded management to invest approximately $1 million to develop a new artificial intelligence (AI) system that would: (1) receive customer calls and attempt to diagnose the problems, (2) provide a solution to the problem (for the customer to implement) or route the call to a support technician, and (3) track the status and performance metrics for each call.

Though the AI system had been under development for more than a year, it was not yet completed and the company's service capability continued to deteriorate rapidly. The company's senior management asked an outside expert to examine the AI development project and to make recommendations to help alleviate the continuing downward spiral in customer service.

After reviewing the project, the expert found that: (1) the AI development project was significantly behind schedule and over budget, and (2) a far simpler approach could be implemented if, in fact, core business issues were addressed more directly.

Working with client support technicians to understand the nature and volume of customer support calls, the outside expert prepared a Pareto analysis (80/20 analysis) to determine the nature of customer support needs. As a result of the analysis, the company was able to identify and fix most of the fundamental underlying business process issues that were causing the real bottlenecks. The company subsequently halted development of the AI system. Not only was the AI system far behind schedule and over budget, but it failed to address several key business issues driving customer support calls.

A comparison of support fees versus calls made to the technical support line indicated that a small number of customers, nearly all of whom paid very little in support fees, generated well over half the calls. These customers tied up phone lines and support capacity, preventing customers who paid far more in support fees from accessing the support technicians, thereby increasing the frustration among the company's largest, best, and most profitable customers. Analysis of the calls found that many resulted from new versions of the software, at times reflecting inadequate testing and user training.

Finally, customers were using more than a dozen versions of the software because no formal upward migration requirement or upgrade program existed. This made it more difficult for technicians to accurately diagnose and fix problems.

Based on this examination, the company decided to make several changes in its relationship with customers. A planned upward migration schedule was established for all customers, and the requirements to upgrade at specific intervals were made a formal part of the customer agreement. Customers were required to update software periodically to minimize the number of versions in the field.

Customers who were not willing to work within the new guidelines were required to pay a premium for support services, compared with customers who got on board with the new program. Product testing was bolstered. Customer training was expanded and improved, which also provided an additional revenue stream.

A tracking system was developed and implemented for all customer calls. High volume users of technical support were tracked, evaluated, and notified if usage appeared to be excessive.

All of these steps improved customer service response time, which, in turn, helped the company gain new business. In hindsight, the CEO and board determined that these issues should have been explored before the company embarked on the AI "solution."

Strategic Failures

Generally, a strategic failure can be attributed directly to poor executive management decisions. Strategic failures tend to have very far-reaching and deep impact on a company.

For example, the following would be considered a strategic failure: A CEO decides to pursue a large merger or a series of acquisitions without conducting adequate IT due diligence, and the resulting integration fails to deliver the expected IT and business synergies, economies of scale, and cost savings. This decision leads to a drop in the company's stock price.

Failure to include all of the necessary functional skills upfront in the acquisition process and to solicit input from IT about the feasibility, cost, and risks of integrating all of the target company's technology within an acceptable time frame is a strategic mistake on the part of the CEO or business-unit leaders.

Attempts by the CEO or other executives to restrict or withhold incremental resources or funding (including IT resources) during a period of major change—for example, during an acquisition or postacquisition period—should be classified as strategic mistakes that can lead to strategic failures and result in business interruptions or failures to achieve results, causing shareholder value to decline.

CASE STUDY 4.7

Choosing a Tailored Solution

A company whose primary business was the manufacture and distribution of industrial products had for years operated a captive finance company designed to facilitate and finance customers' purchases of its major capital products. A decision had been made to divest the finance company.

But the chairman of the finance company was very concerned that his IT organization would become a major liability in any negotiations and a potential deal breaker. The latest problem was a failed attempt to implement a new lease management system.

The finance company chairman, who held other financial positions in the parent company, asked an outside advisor to review the situation and make recommendations about what it would take to stabilize the current IT environment and put in place the professional IT capability and management processes necessary to convince a buyer that things were under control at the finance company. By his own admission, IT was not the chairman's strong suit, and he did not feel the head of IT communicated well with him about the realities of the situation the IT organization faced.

The lease management system had been a packaged solution. User requirements had not been adequately defined before the software purchase, resulting in modifications of more than 60 percent of the package's basic code. The head of IT was forced to hire the software company to do the implementation, driving up both the time and cost. Because the software company lacked experience in conducting implementations, many of the modifications were not adequately tested before going live. As a result, when the system conversion occurred, the integrity of the lease database was questionable.

The absence of an auditable lease database caused the chairman considerable difficulty in moving his divestiture strategy forward on schedule.

An outside advisor worked to stabilize the newly converted leasing system and restore the integrity of the leasing database. This involved conducting numerous account reconciliations and assessing and improving the overall quality and accuracy of the lease database. The company was able to regain control of a very important part of the business and put its divestiture strategy back on track. Additionally, the advisor helped the chairman to engineer the restructuring of the overall IT organization.

In addition to the economic gain for the parent company that resulted from the divestiture of the finance company, corporate leadership learned valuable lessons concerning the control of IT investments and implementations, which resulted in a new approach to managing IT investments across the enterprise.

Massive Infrastructure Failures

Infrastructure failures occur when the fundamental physical utility aspects of an IT organization break down. Such breakdowns can occur in networks, routers, servers, PCs, or other hardware and system software. If the IT people responsible for the infrastructure cannot restore service in the necessary time frame, severe business interruption and loss of shareholder value results. The inability of IT operations staff to implement the necessary technical management tools and processes to effectively monitor the performance of the infrastructure and prevent or immediately deal with problems is one of the most frequent causes of massive infrastructure failure.

In industries and businesses heavily dependent on real-time, high-volume transaction processing (e.g., financial services, retail, online information services), a massive infrastructure failure will cause an immediate halt to operations and result in immediate revenue losses. Even a short interruption in businesses of this type because of infrastructure failure will typically create an immediate crisis in confidence in the marketplace and potentially cause a drop in stock price.

Very often, massive infrastructure failures occur because of a lack of attention to or funding of redundancy and backup/recovery processes. If businesses that are heavily dependent on infrastructure lack sufficient redundancy and automated backup and recovery procedures, any failure can almost be considered a strategic failure; someone who should have been thinking about these things missed the big picture.

Continued intermittent infrastructure failures will drive customers away permanently and result in earnings decay, a lack of shareholder confidence, and a decrease in shareholder value. In addition, chronic IT problems and infrastructure failures will cause some of the highest, most volatile levels of business-unit leader and user frustration with IT simply because infrastructure is what everyone sees, is touched by, and depends on every day.

CASE STUDY 4.8

Integrate or Pay the Price

A leading financial information company providing online, time-dependent securities trading and pricing information was embarking on a strategy to expand its portfolio of products and services. The first new product line it was seeking to develop and roll out to the marketplace was a specialized type of bond trading product.

Over a period of 18 months, the company had made significant investments in this new product. However, the company had already embarrassed itself in the marketplace by releasing the product prematurely—that is, before the technology base on which it had been built had been adequately tested. This false start occurred after the head of IT, against his better judgment, succumbed to severe pressure from the CEO and bond-product business-unit leader to meet an unreasonable release deadline and to allow the product to be offered without having adequately tested the supporting technology infrastructure.

As a result, on the first day of the product's release, the volume of traffic on the system was so high that it was brought to its knees, creating unacceptable response times, screen blackouts and lock-ups, and frustrated customers. The CEO, who was very apologetic to his customers and somewhat chagrined, immediately pulled the product off the market.

Although this was a huge blow for the otherwise highly rated, top-performing company, it was something the company could weather by approaching damage control, recovery, and rerelease properly. From an IT perspective, a complete meltdown had occurred, both technically and organizationally. The IT infrastructure had buckled under the stress.

The hierarchical and siloed structure of the IT organization that had been in place had worked reasonably well for the company in the past, when all of its products and services were fairly narrow and addressed single-channel markets and customers. However, delivering this new product required many parts of the business, including the IT organization, to cross traditional functional boundaries.

Some of these coordination and hand-off points were more than simply ragged. The business people, most of whom had little experience with products of this type and nature, severely underestimated the volume requirements. Because the IT people had not worked together as a fully coordinated team, they did not press the issue as hard as they should have. In the end, the CEO's drive to force the product out too quickly and his naiveté about technology-based product rollouts, including infrastructure requirements, created a disaster waiting to happen.

The end result was a product that was supposed to have been completed and earning revenue for the company six months earlier but was still in its final stages of restructuring, including a major infrastructure overhaul.

In addition, the CEO began seriously to question his IT leader's capability, judgment, and overall business acumen. The reality was that although the IT leader had thus far been able to cope with the business, he was now attempting to work several levels above his capability—the company had simply outgrown his competencies. For obvious reasons, the CEO was deathly afraid to rerelease the product and possibly have it fail a second time. Not only would a second failure kill the product and its future revenue streams, but it would create major questions in the marketplace about the company's reputation and even its ongoing viability.

Recognizing his predicament, the CEO turned outside for assistance. He could not afford to make the same mistake twice. He brought in an expert to assess the readiness of the restructured product to be rereleased into the marketplace. He wanted to be certain that it could handle the planned volume.

The expert devised a unique simulation testing process involving multiple customer and user scenarios. During the testing process, the product was taken to its breaking point, and appropriate measurements, IT management processes, and "safety valves" were put in place to ensure that ongoing monitoring would be available to prevent another failure.

The restructured product was released as promised, and the company regained its image in the marketplace. In fact, the manner in which the company approached the restructuring and rerelease of the product was considered a model in the industry, enhancing the company's reputation. However, this massive infrastructure (and strategy) failure had cost the company at least six months of revenue and doubled what it had planned to spend.

Shortly after the rerelease, the CEO commissioned a program to reorganize and restructure the IT organization from top to bottom. The impact to the business of the product failure was substantial, and although the company fully recovered, the CEO never again underestimated the need to fully integrate IT into the company's business planning. Nor did he underestimate the impact IT could have on the company's value.

Security Failures

Security failures can affect any organization and occur for a variety of reasons, ranging from a lack of security policies or lax enforcement of such policies to ineffective security practices or a culture not attuned to security. They can even occur because of direct sabotage from inside or outside the organization. For whatever reasons, security failures can devastate a company and bring it to its knees in a number of ways, both operationally and financially.

For example, if an individual breaches a company's security by penetrating a firewall and installs a virus that takes down every server and PC, the company loses customer confidence, general business reputation, and real money. Or, if a hacker breaks into a company's network and steals credit card numbers stored from Internet sales, the company will have serious financial and customer confidence problems.

Many security problems originate with disgruntled IT (or other) employees who hold the keys to private company data and decide to cause damage or steal valuable information that they can sell when they leave the company. In fact, whereas cases involving external hackers receive the most publicity, internal security breaches are far more common and, in some ways, more dangerous.

In all of these scenarios, security failures, like other types of failures, can cause many kinds of business interruptions and negatively impact shareholders. The embarrassment factor alone from a major security failure can cause a CEO to lose his or her job, permanently tarnish a company's image, and drive customers to walk away in droves.

CASE STUDY 4.9

Dealing with the Threat Within

A new COO was appointed to oversee the international sales and distribution operations of a major American company that manufactured heavy machinery and related products. Having been with the company for many years, the new COO was aware of the IT problems that had historically plagued this division, problems that included major concerns about the competency of the IT leader and his immediate management team.

An internationally seasoned and very pragmatic executive, the COO was committed from the start to improving the business unit's IT situation. However, he realized he would need significant outside professional resources to help him create a set of focused improvement plans.

For many years, the company had taken advantage of beneficial tax arrangements by basing its international sales and distribution in Western Europe. For a long period, the company had also made many unsuccessful attempts to implement an integrated international order, sales, and distribution system.

These efforts resulted in an IT landscape that can best be described as cobbled together, an eclectic mix of partially completed systems that required significant manual intervention to process transactions. The highly fragmented nature of this aging mix of largely undocumented software islands created a high-cost, high-maintenance environment. Major gaps in security were also a problem.

From the IT director's perspective, this situation guaranteed him and his immediate management team perpetual employment. As long as the current situation existed, they would be the only ones inside or outside the company who could maintain the system. Unfortunately, they also knew how poor the security really was.

However, in the COO's mind, such a situation placed the company in a hostage situation, especially as the IT director and his team became more and more aggressive in making demands on the company. The IT director exacerbated this already intolerable situation by threatening to crash the system unless the company did what he wanted. For the COO, this was the final straw.

The COO asked his outside advisors to provide him with a team of highly skilled IT professionals, experienced in management and control, systems development, IT and physical security, business recovery, and crisis management to assist him in wresting control of the IT operations from the IT director. He asked the team, which worked directly for him, to develop and execute a secure exit plan for the IT director and key members of his management team and a comprehensive stabilization program to protect the integrity and security of the company's systems.

An IT security team determined that although a number of very significant security weaknesses existed, with effort, it would be possible to establish a secure enough environment to protect the company's assets once the IT director and his team were gone.

A second team focused on documentation and business continuity issues associated with the old, fragmented software systems and hardware platforms. This team confirmed the systems' fragility but, nonetheless, was able to establish enough overview documentation to considerably reduce the risk of business interruption.

Working directly with the COO in strictest confidence, the experts developed an appropriate exit plan that involved the rapid removal of the IT director and selected members of his team and a full resecuring of the overall

IT environment. Even with a well-thought-out and very swiftly executed plan, certain members of the IT director's inner circle still attempted to sabotage the IT infrastructure and key applications. However, these attempts were thwarted because of the advance precautions the security team had taken just before removing the IT director.

The exit, security, and system protection plans were executed simultaneously, enabling the COO to move forward with his business and IT plans for the division without any adverse effects.

From this experience, corporate leaders realized that IT operations, security, and control issues needed to be elevated throughout the company to ensure that the significant investments being made were being managed and monitored effectively and were helping rather than hindering the business.

WHAT THE CEO CAN DO TO ENSURE THAT THE IT ORGANIZATION IS ALIGNED WITH THE BUSINESS'S PROFITABILITY DRIVERS

Alignment of the IT organization with the business's profitability drivers must occur if IT is to fulfill its promise to add value to the business. In fact, even the most cost-effective and efficient IT organizations cannot compensate for not having an organization in place that is structured to enable itself to be regularly reshaped and transformed in response to changing business objectives.

CEOs can take five concrete steps to ensure that their company's IT organization is agile, flexible, and adaptive enough to deal with constant change:

1. Make sure that the CIO fully understands the major drivers of profitability and shareholder value for the company, can draw the link between these drivers and IT, and can clearly articulate that link.
2. With the CIO, develop a presentation to the executive management team and the board highlighting exactly how the IT organization is structured to handle change in a focused and cost-effective manner.
3. Have the CIO work together with the head of HR to develop an IT organization career model that is focused on its specific needs and those of the company as a whole.

4. Ask the CIO to prepare a presentation that sufficiently details how he or she has addressed the four major IT failure risks that can affect earnings, profitability drivers, and shareholder value—*execution failure, strategic failure, massive infrastructure failure, and security failure.* Make sure that the CIO's plans contain real substance in this regard.

5. Include the CIO in strategic scenario planning sessions and regularly engage him or her in a dialogue concerning different strategic scenarios for the business; solicit his or her views as to how the IT organization would respond based on these scenarios.

Understand the *Real* IT Spend

Measuring the Impact of IT Costs

A global financial services company was considering lending money to a private equity firm to support its acquisition of a large direct marketing company that served millions of customers through more than two dozen carefully managed marketing campaigns. The private equity firm had already done its due diligence on the target company. However, because of the essential role information technology plays in such an operation, the potential lender sought a second opinion about the target company's IT environment to make sure it was adequate to support operations, sales, and marketing.

Of particular importance to the lender was validation of potential cost savings identified by the target company. In addition, a number of IT projects underway suggested that some issues existed surrounding the stability of the system.

The outside advisor's analysis addressed:

- Reasonableness of operating and capital expenditures related to IT, including a review of the company's forward-looking capital expenditures budget and identification of potential opportunities for reduction in expenditures.
- Adequacy of the existing IT environment used to support the company's operations, including its resilience and business continuity planning.

- Sufficiency of the company's information systems used for sales, marketing, and mailing activities.
- Major IT infrastructure and applications projects and/or initiatives underway or planned that could potentially affect the stability of the company's existing IT environment.

As a result of the analysis, the outside advisor told the financial services company that it should not expect the target company to achieve any short-term reductions in IT costs, given the state of the company's implementation plans.

With this advice in hand, the financial services company modified its financial models to reflect the impact of delayed cost savings and established a process for monitoring progress on implementation of a mission-critical distribution system. The company and the private equity firm renegotiated the terms of the loan, and the deal was successfully completed.

It is a common mistake to overestimate cost savings and synergies with respect to IT. In this case, the individuals involved did not originally understand the "real" IT spend associated with the integration and had the projected cost savings not been adjusted downward before conclusion of the deal, they would have severely overstated their potential savings—and the overall value of the deal.

The key to budgeting for IT is not how much is spent, but how wisely it is spent. Current IT budgeting in many companies is haphazard at best. Survey after survey of CEOs and CFOs point to IT cost overruns and ballooning IT budgets as a source of irritation, frustration, and mistrust. Another source of irritation is a perceived lack of quality in the delivery of IT services.

Partly to blame for this apparent disconnect between IT costs and service is a lack of transparent pricing mechanisms for IT services. Few IT organizations actually operate with a separate P&L, and most do not charge actual cash to operating business units or corporate departments for the services they provide. Without the ability of users to actually consider the costs of maintaining an IT environment in terms of real money, the IT organization becomes a sort of black box into which corporate and business-unit funding pours and out of which flows a service that never quite seems to meet the hype with which it is presented to corporate and business-unit decision makers. (Another aspect of the problem involves a lack of manageable performance metrics for IT, which is the subject of the next chapter.)

Many companies simply do not know in any sort of detail or with any accuracy what IT assets they own, where those assets reside, and how much it costs to run them on an ongoing basis. (IT assets can include hardware, software, networks, services, and people.) Until the asset base is determined, users and executives at the business-unit and corporate level cannot fully appreciate the amount of resources required just to maintain these IT assets, especially as they age.

Business-unit executives often implement technology solutions to address various business issues without in any way projecting the ongoing costs of maintaining those systems. Many times, they do not appreciate the costs associated with possible switchovers to more robust systems or to newly available companywide systems. Over time, responsibility for maintaining this spaghetti of legacy IT infrastructure and systems throughout the company drifts over to the IT organization, along with the associated costs, taking up more and more of IT's staff time and delaying important implementations of new and more cost-effective technology.

According to a recent Giga report by Forrester analyst Marc Cercere, "For many reasons, IT shops are attempting to reduce costs, or at least reduce growth of IT costs. CIOs are increasingly expected to run IT as a business and understand business direction and processes. In addition, senior managers outside of IT are learning how technology can be used; but at the same time they need to understand the limitations of IT and the costs associated with IT. The lack of this understanding results in naïve expectations with regard to the time and cost of implementation and end results."*

To properly budget its IT operations, a company should take a "snapshot" of its IT assets, understand the costs associated with those assets, and think about how those funds might be better allocated. Then, it should develop a forward-looking budget. In many cases, components of these assets do not reside within the boundaries of the IT organization and are

---

* *IT Trends 2003: Organizational Design.* Giga Information Group, Inc. (October 8, 2002).

hidden deep in the fiber of various corporate departments and operating business units.

Over time, as these assets are identified, rationalized, and standardized, the budgeting process for the company's total IT spend will become more robust, detailed, and on target and will provide more accurate baselines for investment, ROI, and comparative benchmarking analyses.

One large, well-managed company thought it had outstanding control over its IT spend and asset base. During an intense due-diligence process after it had been acquired by a smaller, more nimble competitor, it was discovered that more than 40 percent of the company's IT spend and asset base actually resided outside what was officially reported as IT. These IT assets and expenditures were hidden deep within the company's business units, primarily because the business units were not being properly serviced by the corporate and divisional IT groups. Thus, the business units had taken matters into their own hands and, over time, had built up multiple, individual, ad-hoc IT capabilities. To hide this fact, they simply called the IT expenditures they were making by various other names. The business units were not getting what they needed and decided to take the path of least resistance to *fix* IT, duplicating numerous base IT costs and investments along the way.

BUILD THE IT BUDGET

An IT budget can be built in one of two ways: from the top down ("This is how much money we have to spend, now how do we spend it?") or from the bottom up ("These are the things we need to do in IT, and these are the things we would like to do. Now how much will it cost?").

Whichever approach is used, before a realistic forward-looking IT budget can be developed, the company needs to define the specific technologies, systems, activities, processes, and people that will become part of the budget that the CIO and the IT organization own or are responsible to deliver on behalf of the company and those that will be managed by others outside the IT organization. In either case, IT budgeting cannot be performed in a vacuum. It must directly involve, include, and engage all constituencies to ensure appropriate ownership of and accountability for the key IT budget drivers and spend items. To accomplish this, a company must determine:

- How much is currently spent on IT in the IT department's own budget, and how much is hidden away in business-unit operating budgets under IT or non-IT line items. This is called *total spend analysis* (TSA).

- How the drivers of this total spend will be allocated in the future, what properly goes into the IT budget, and what properly stays in operating budgets of the business units. This involves deciding the *ownership* of the IT spend.

- Who is responsible for executing the activities and tasks associated with the spending. Sometimes the execution is divided between the CIO's organization and the business unit. Sometimes it helps to have an outside third party take on the responsibility for execution. However, someone in the company, either in the IT organization or in a business unit, must still assume overall accountability for the spend.

- The IT budget for "must have" activities. If budgeting is performed from the top down, the company must determine if it is feasible to maintain all current IT activities at current service levels or to make trade-offs by eliminating activities or reducing service levels. If budgeting is bottom up or if there is money left over in a top-down budgeting exercise, after taking into account operation of all the must haves at their current service levels or possibly even improving those service levels, a company must rank the *desires* for future IT spending by all constituencies. If the proposed budget exceeds the available funding, hard decisions must be made collectively by the business units, the IT organization, and corporate executives about what stays in the budget and what goes. This is often a highly emotional and politically charged exercise. However, it must be done, and the CIO must drive this process and directly involve corporate and business-unit leadership. This is called *ruthless prioritization*.

One company I worked with had created an elaborate, elegant forms-driven IT budgeting process that mirrored the overall formal corporate budgeting process. Everyone dutifully completed the forms, and an IT budget was created. On the surface, it appeared that all IT expenditures had to go through a rigorous review before being approved. However, at the same time, everyone knew that the IT budget continued to grow disproportionately to the company's ability to support it. The problem was that over time, *form* had overtaken *substance* in the IT budgeting process, and nobody was really "getting behind" the numbers in an effort to understand the real intent and value of the planned IT investments and expenditures. The IT prioritization process had lost the intensity, focus, and objectivity it needed to be helpful to the business.

ANALYZE THE CURRENT SPEND

IT spending typically falls into one of five categories. Some involve both capital expenditures and the costs of ongoing operations, services, and maintenance, whereas others involve only the costs associated with ongoing operations, services, and maintenance. In all categories, the costs of physical assets, as well as the costs of human resources, must be fully considered. The five categories are:

1. The IT infrastructure, which might be considered the *utility* aspects of IT. This includes PCs, basic PC software, peripherals, servers, networks and telecommunications, Internet connectivity, support/help desks, and break/fix maintenance.

These infrastructure elements should be owned by the IT organization on behalf of the business units. The business units should own the specific cost drivers associated with these items because they are directly related to a combination of the number of employees in the unit, the volume of usage, and any special needs the unit has. This is typically the easiest area in which an IT organization operating on a *profit center* or Gartner-style ISCo (internal services company) model can establish a transparent charge-back or transfer pricing system for business units.

2. PC-specific functional and business-unit software tools. These include software licenses, leases, additional hardware, special support, or help desks dedicated to software used by a particular corporate function (e.g., human resources) or a particular business unit (e.g., the book publishing unit of a multidivision publishing company, which must pay royalties to authors instead of one-time checks to magazine or newspaper writers). Also included in this category is the money spent on IT or on other business-unit staff resources to directly support these tools.

PC-specific functional and business-unit software tools are usually owned by the business unit (i.e., included in the business-unit's budget) and executed jointly by the IT organization and the function or business unit. Typically, however, the IT organization provides services and support for these special items on behalf of the business-unit or functional department. IT can "bill" the department or business unit specifically for the human resources it puts on the job, the special tools it needs to use, or the general IT assets it must use to provide the support.

3. Server- or mainframe-based legacy functional or business-unit applications. These are owned by the function or business unit and executed jointly by the IT organization and the function or business unit. Items in this category include software leases, software maintenance and upgrade contracts, dedicated servers, special network/telecommunications/Internet support, application-specific help desks, and the cost of IT or other business-unit staff resources spent in direct support of these applications. Again, the IT organization can directly "bill" the department or business unit for particular services.

4. New functional and business-unit applications just coming online but not yet operational or mainstream. These include software, additional hardware, and special support or help desks, internal IT and business-unit staff resources, and outside third-party costs. They are owned by the CIO and executed jointly by the IT organization and the functional department or business unit. These items appear on the IT budget.

5. New functional and business-unit application projects. These include transitions from legacy to new systems, software, hardware, infrastructure, and project management, and a number of costs that might include internal IT and business-unit staff resources and outside third parties. These costs are owned by the CIO and executed jointly by the IT organization and the functional department or business unit. Usually, however, the IT organization is asked to execute these projects on behalf of the business unit. These items also appear on the IT budget.

Table 5.1 consolidates the ownership, execution responsibilities, and overall accountability of IT assets.

Why is it important that jointly managed assets owned by the department or business unit be aggregated with the spend for IT organization-owned assets? The answer is threefold.

First, aggregating the spend is the only way to get a clear picture of those costs over which the IT organization actually has control. Remember, the total spend analysis exercise is a part of changing the mind-set of IT users from, "IT is a free service, always there, always perfect" to, "That

Table 5.1 IT Budget/Spend Accountability Overview

IT Spend Area	Ownership of IT Spend Drivers		Responsibility for Execution of IT Spend		Accountability for Overall IT Spend	
	Business Unit	IT	Business Unit	IT	Business Unit	IT
IT Infrastructure* PCs. Basic PC software. Peripherals. Servers. Networks/telecom. Internet connectivity. Support/help desks.	✓	✓		✓	✓	✓
PC-Specific Business Unit Infrastructure and Software Tools Software. Additional hardware. Special support/help desks.	✓		✓		✓	✓
Server/Mainframe-Based Legacy Business Unit Infrastructure and Applications Software leases. Software maintenance and upgrade contracts. Dedicated servers. Special network/telecom/Internet support. Application-specific help desks.	✓	✓	✓	✓	✓	✓
New Business Unit Infrastructure and Applications Transition from legacy to "new" costs. Software. Hardware. Infrastructure. Project management.	✓	✓	✓	✓	✓	✓
New Business Unit Infrastructure and Applications Projects Software. Additional hardware. Special support/help desks.	✓	✓	✓	✓	✓	✓

* Direct or allocated functional portion of IT infrastructure.

service costs money and can be improved or impaired depending on the amount of resources dedicated to it."

Second, capturing these costs—especially the actual incremental costs associated with operating legacy systems—helps the IT organization to assemble business cases, when appropriate, for upgrading hardware, software, and support.

Third, finding what IT assets and resources are residing in departments or business units helps the CIO create a case for standardizing and consolidating purchases as varied as PCs, help desk services, telecommunications network access, and outside services, thereby driving down the company's aggregate IT spend. Today's CIO must have the ability to be able to earn a seat at the executive table and to establish his or her credibility with corporate and business-unit leadership.

CASE STUDY 5.2

Aligning the IT Budget with Company Needs and Objectives

On acquiring another company, a large U.S.-based entertainment firm installed a new CFO/COO in the acquired company's management. This new executive sought to better understand the financial and operational drivers of the business.

Even though much work was done in this area during the due diligence efforts before the deal closed, executive management wanted to validate the financial condition of the acquired company. IT was one of the areas about which the new operating executive was concerned.

During the due diligence effort, the CIO of the acquired company seemed evasive when answering some key questions about the company's IT spend, but because of the deal-closing deadline, further in-depth analysis of IT was delayed until after the acquisition was completed.

During his initial discussions with the CIO, the new CFO/COO continued to feel that the CIO was not telling him everything about the company's IT priorities and overall IT spend and about IT's relationship with the business units. The COO/CFO asked an outside advisor to review the existing IT budget, to provide a realistic assessment of the company's IT spend, and to assess the overall IT organization and its effectiveness.

The advisor attempted to work with the CIO in dissecting and reassembling the IT budget, based on various business scenarios that highlighted different sets of priorities. However, the CIO was very uncooperative. After a short time, it became obvious that the IT budget the CIO had submitted did not really reflect the business units' objectives, and that no real accountability had been built into the budget. In addition, the CIO had not spent any meaningful time working with the business units' executives in trying to understand their critical needs. The budget reflected only the CIO's views of what he thought the business units should have rather than what they actually needed.

After learning this, the new CFO/COO removed the CIO and asked the advisor to work directly with the executives of each of the business units to come to an understanding of their key business issues and priorities. The COO/CFO demanded an objective and accurate picture of the company's IT needs, as well as the resulting IT budget requirements.

Over time, the IT budget was deconstructed, examined as to the strategic fit of various IT assets and future IT needs, and reassembled. As a result of this analysis, the COO/CFO was able to redirect and streamline the IT budget. A number of the larger IT projects were put on hold by the parent company, and the budget that had been allocated for these projects was freed up. Greater fiscal and operational control was embedded into both the IT organization and the business units. A new budgeting process was established and implemented, together with appropriate IT management and fiscal processes and new measurements.

Business-unit management became more involved in the IT planning and prioritization process, and IT budgets and projects were better focused on key business priorities. At the conclusion of this exercise, the IT budget more accurately reflected and realistically represented the company's total IT spend and was a far wiser budget.

DETERMINE WHO OWNS AND EXECUTES EACH ITEM OF THE SPEND

Owners of the IT spend—those accountable for meeting expectations of quality, timeliness, and meeting the budget—are determined by those who own the drivers of the spend items and those who deliver the services.

Sometimes, the IT organization clearly owns the drivers, either because it is best able to handle pure technology issues or because the IT organization is wholly responsible for the activity. Other times, the business unit clearly owns the drivers, but the IT organization provides the service on behalf of the business unit.

A third scenario occurs when the IT organization and the business unit jointly own the drivers. An example of such a scenario is where the IT organization provides basic PC support services for everyone in the company. In this case, the business unit owns the primary cost drivers related to class and power of PC, software required, number of users, volume of e-mail traffic, and so on. However, the IT organization owns the drivers related to cost-effective provision of services, such as overall PC procurement contract/unit pricing, help desk productivity, network efficiency, and so on.

In most cases of this kind, the business units will have ceded responsibility to the IT organization to provide common PC support services in a standardized manner across the company. Ultimately, the IT organization has responsibility for delivering the agreed-on or budgeted per-unit or per-head IT spend for these services. The IT organization and the business units must jointly own the IT spend because to manage it, each must fulfill its obligations to the other. For example, if a business unit's head count increases substantially because of unplanned growth or an acquisition, the IT organization cannot be expected to provide the same level of service at the same total cost to the expanded operating unit. The IT organization must be able to add the number and type of resources necessary to deliver the same level of service.

If the business unit cannot afford to spend more at that time, the only choice is to accept a lower level of service. In such a case, business–unit leadership must take the responsibility for the decision to reduce the service level and not allow business-unit users to blame the IT organization for the lower level of service. However, if the IT organization is not meeting its obligations to provide the agreed-on service levels at the agreed-on cost, it needs to be held accountable for not performing.

The process of sorting out accountability—not as a means of beating up one party or the other, but as a way to identify problems and develop solutions—can flourish only in an atmosphere of healthy, open dialog between the IT organization and its operating business unit or corporate departmental constituencies. Without such dialog, joint accountability becomes difficult to manage, finger pointing increases, and progress stagnates.

In still other cases, a business unit might own a greater portion of the IT spend because it may be unilaterally sponsoring a special IT effort that is totally unique to the business unit. For example, if a business unit were developing its own Web-based customer service application, it might cede full responsibility for delivering the service to the IT organization or it might contract with an outside provider on its own or through the IT organization.

Either way, even though the business unit has greater responsibility for the spend, it still has to depend on the IT organization to ensure that the system works compatibly on company-standard PCs, servers, and networks, and it may also have to provide services for the system. As well, the CIO needs to include the item in the total IT spend analysis he or she is required to provide to his or her executive-level peers.

If dialogue between the IT organization and business unit or corporate department partners breaks down, unsanctioned, hidden, and shadow IT costs build up in pockets around the company; overall service declines; and business-unit leaders, users, and members of the IT organization become frustrated. Continuous IT organization/business-unit dialogue and business-focused decision making must continue to ensure that priorities are set based on key business-unit objectives and on their ability to spend to meet those objectives.

At one company with which I worked, I was asked to play the Solomon role between two warring factions—the CIO and IT organization and the CEOs of the business units. They could not agree in an adult manner on who owned the IT spend and budget for the company, and an ever-escalating argument was raging.

The main problem was that their misplaced focus was exclusively on the IT spend amounts rather than on the underlying drivers of the spend. Business units contended that IT had to own its spend, and IT insisted that business units needed to accept some responsibility for the spend. After several weeks locked away with a small group, I finally got them to understand and focus on the spend drivers and on whose actions—IT, business unit, or both—could affect these drivers, rather than just on the spend amount itself. In the end, they realized that it was not an either/or situation and that each group actually had some level of ownership over different actions that impacted the various components of IT spend. In addition, they also realized that the only way for them to get their IT spend under control was to work on it together as a team at a granular *driver* level.

No single predefined formula exists for determining who owns the IT cost drivers, the execution, and the IT spend itself. These are dependent on the dynamics of the individual company. However, basic principles can be followed when preparing the IT budget:

- A driver of the IT spend should be owned primarily by the group (i.e., the IT organization, a business unit, a corporate department) that has the most effect on the driver.
- To the extent possible, maximum control over the spend should be put in the hands of the people who are users of the service, whether standard or specialized. If people own the control and know that they are paying for that for which they've asked, ultimately, they will help control the spend.
- IT spend can be owned jointly by the IT organization and the business unit or department, but a formal activity-based service level agreement (SLA) should be in place for the cost drivers and service execution and delivery levels.
- Total spend analyses covering all costs to the company (rather than narrowly focused on point-in-time costs) must be employed when analyzing IT costs and service levels to ensure full transparency.
- Continuous dialogue and constant liaison between the IT organization and the business unit or department must exist to ensure that changes in either group that might affect the SLA are discussed candidly and that all options, costs, benefits, and risks are fully transparent.
- The keys to achieving full transparency in the IT budget are to develop and use appropriate and relevant IT performance and value measurements.

Typically, an IT budget can be divided into five major spend categories (Figure 5.1):

1. *Business-unit-driven IT costs:* Independent/discreet business unit needs requested of and addressed by the IT organization on behalf of a business unit, including activities such as PC procurement, installation and maintenance of dedicated servers, and special applications work. This category is by far the largest in terms of costs, often accounting for roughly 50 percent of a company's total IT spend.
2. *IT operations and management base costs:* Primarily IT staffing costs and the structure necessary to support IT staff, as well as the IT financial and

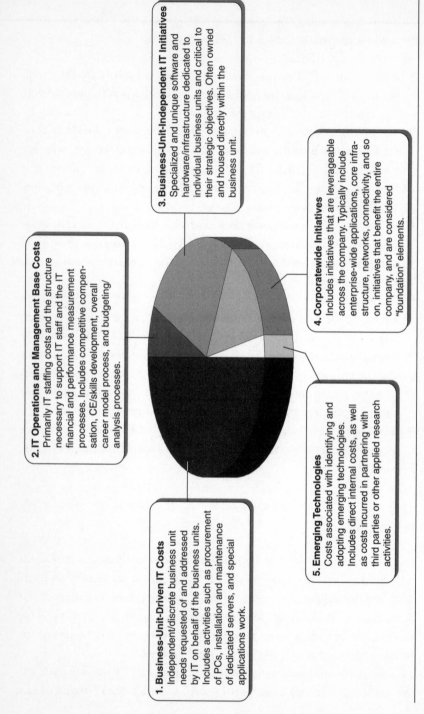

2. IT Operations and Management Base Costs
Primarily IT staffing costs and the structure necessary to support IT staff and the IT financial and performance measurement processes. Includes competitive compensation, CE/skills development, overall career model process, and budgeting/analysis processes.

3. Business-Unit-Independent IT Initiatives
Specialized and unique software and hardware/infrastructure dedicated to individual business units and critical to their strategic objectives. Often owned and housed directly within the business unit.

4. Corporatewide Initiatives
Includes initiatives that are leverageable across the company. Typically include enterprise-wide applications, core infrastructure, networks, connectivity, and so on, initiatives that benefit the entire company, and are considered "foundation" elements.

1. Business-Unit-Driven IT Costs
Independent/discrete business unit needs requested of and addressed by IT on behalf of the business units. Includes activities such as procurement of PCs, installation and maintenance of dedicated servers, and special applications work.

5. Emerging Technologies
Costs associated with identifying and adopting emerging technologies. Includes direct internal costs, as well as costs incurred in partnering with third parties or other applied research activities.

Figure 5.1 Overview of IT Budget/Spend Categories.

performance measurement processes. These include competitive compensation, continuing education and skills development, the overall career model process, and the budgeting/analysis processes.

3. *Business-unit-independent IT initiatives:* Specialized and unique software and hardware infrastructure dedicated to individual business units and to their strategic objectives. These are often owned and housed within the business unit.

4. *Corporatewide initiatives:* Includes initiatives that can be leveraged across the company. These typically include enterprisewide applications, core infrastructure, networks, connectivity, and other initiatives that benefit the entire company and that are considered *foundation* elements.

5. *Emerging technologies:* Costs associated with identifying, experimenting with, and adopting emerging technologies, including direct internal costs as well as costs incurred in partnering with third parties or in engaging in other applied research activities.

MAKE CUTS IN SCOPE OR SERVICE LEVEL IF NECESSARY

In a bottom-up budgeting environment, before a company can decide what it wants to add to its current IT portfolio, it must determine if it is doing the right things and doing things right. This means determining if the company's basic needs for IT support are being met and if the service levels provided by IT to users are good enough.

This issue is most significant in a top-down budgeting environment. The questions are: Is the amount of money arbitrarily allocated for the IT organization sufficient to provide the desired support at the desired service levels? If not, what support will be canceled and which service levels will be allowed to degrade?

To get at the issue of appropriate services and service levels, a number of questions need to be asked. Five questions for the bottom-up budgeter are:

1. What is the service being provided?
2. What are the current services being provided?
3. Should the service level be improved?
4. Should services be added?
5. Are all services necessary, and must they be provided at the current service level?

For the top-down budgeter, the following four questions are relevant:

1. How much money is available for IT services?
2. What services must be provided in that budget?
3. What level of service can be provided in the budget, given the number of services that must be provided?
4. Who will provide the service (internal resources—the IT organization, the business unit, or the department—or external resources)? What are the cost differences?

When the discussion is framed in this way, consumers of IT services can better see the real cost associated with the IT organization's providing a particular service. When the IT organization is considered a service provider and not merely a cost center, users can more easily view it as analogous to an outside provider of services that resides within the company. The discussion between the CIO and company leadership that consumes IT services (business units and corporate functional departments) can be more at arm's length. The CIO can say, in effect, "Tell me what you need and tell me what you want. I'll tell you what it will cost."

Help-desk support for PC users offers a very clear example of an area in which service levels can be defined, measured, and priced.

Everyone is comfortable with the notion that a customer cannot buy a coach-class airline seat and then demand to be seated in first class, where he or she will receive first-class service. Everyone is also comfortable with the notion that verified overnight delivery of an item sent through the U.S. Postal Service commands a premium price. These realities conform to the idea that "nothing is free" or that "you get what you pay for."

Why then do educated, savvy business professionals, well aware of the laws of economics and fully willing in their private lives to pay for the level of service they desire, expect that these principles do not exist for corporate IT services? For some reason, a myth has grown up in many companies that unlimited funds are available for IT and that people can always ask for "more" and "better" without having to pay for the additional costs.

By always trying to please everyone and minimize complaints, IT organizations are, perhaps, partly to blame for this misperception. Even so, the days of the IT free ride are over. Given the level of IT spend in most companies today and the elusiveness of the IT promise of massive productivity

gains and synergies, a direct correlation must be drawn between IT spend
and service levels. Everyone is responsible for helping to manage toward a
wise IT spend.

Figure 5.2 illustrates how different drivers (class of use/service level
and the speed/availability of the service) work together to increase cost.

Today's CIO is responsible for making sure that everyone in the company, from executive management and business-unit leaders to users at all
levels, understands the impact of their IT service decisions on the total IT
spend. Typically, the IT service-spend/cost equation can be simplified by
creating what are called classes of use/service categories across all areas of
the IT spend.

Class of use/service is generally driven by the complexity or volume of
the use/service required. In the interest of simplicity and transparency, a
company should limit the number of classes. Doing so helps drive standardization and increase cost efficiency and economies of scale. Another component of the service-spend equation is speed and availability: How quickly
must the service be delivered? How universal must the availability be?

Business units that can live with standard service levels at normal
speeds—for instance, a mature business unit with well-developed processes
and little change in its business model over time—pay the least per unit of

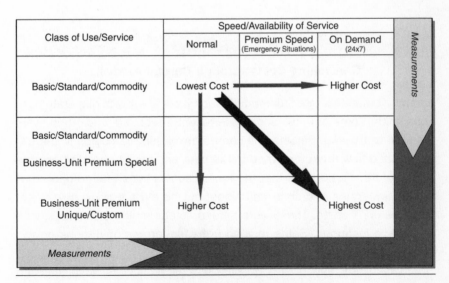

Figure 5.2   IT Spend/Budget Drivers.

volume or per head. Other business units, which require highly customized or unique types of service and very fast delivery of these services at any time—for instance, a fast-growing business unit with a highly mobile workforce—pay the most per unit of volume or per head. For these business units, revenues must fully support their needs or, to cover their costs, they will be forced to find increased investment funds or to obtain a corporate subsidy.

Such an approach allows all business units and corporate departments to share in basic, standard, commodity-type services at the same unit cost, the driver being either the number of users or the volume of use by class of use or service. Business units or departments requiring higher levels of more specialized services and/or a faster speed or greater availability can identify the premium services they want and buy them from the IT organization "by the pound" in increments above the standard services.

The process described here follows a *value for money* model; everyone can see and control what they receive and how it is delivered. This increases each business unit's feeling of trust and control over its IT destiny. Constructing the IT budget and measurement process around this model creates a win-win scenario across the board. The foundation for achieving the win-win is a carefully- and responsibly-crafted SLA that forces all parties to sign on the dotted line and to be accountable to one another.

CASE STUDY 5.3

Controlling Costs through Careful Analysis

A new CIO was appointed for a multinational company with disparate business units. Some of these units were recently acquired, and others were targeted to be sold. Because he came from within the company, the CIO understood how it had operated in the past and how it hoped to operate in the future. He believed that the recent acquisitions offered opportunities for synergies and cost reductions, but he did not know how to get a handle on IT costs. These were spread across multiple business units in multiple locations. Some resided in headquarter's operations on two continents.

To make progress toward achieving any cost reductions, he needed first to understand the current IT asset base and where money was being spent.

He sought assistance to help him focus on the current desktop environment (e.g., PCs, services, networks, support/help desk, and break/fix maintenance), which supported many thousands of users in corporate headquarters and in local business-unit locations.

Data was collected about the current desktop environment, focusing on current support and service costs (labor) and procurement and maintenance costs for hardware and software, including PCs and related server and network components. Data was evaluated in the context of the company's operations and measured against industry norms. It was discovered that a number of factors were driving higher than expected costs. These included:

- A high number of premium users who made frequent calls for support
- A higher than warranted level of service for those premium users
- The need to dispatch deskside technical staff for a large number of relatively low-level support requests as well as more complex requests
- An inability to set and follow established, standard, predefined, and agreed-on criteria for prioritizing and providing desktop service requests.

The outside advisor who helped with the analysis recommended a five-point improvement program to address the current deficiencies and achieve a future vision for more effective desktop support. He also made project recommendations and established a schedule for implementation. The plan showed cost savings within three months.

FOCUS ON TOTAL AND LIFETIME SPEND

IT budgets are too often prepared as if every IT initiative were being developed in a vacuum. This type of budgeting presumes that an IT initiative goes through a development period and then is magically implemented without any extra costs to overall system maintenance. Would that it were so.

In reality, linking any IT initiative into the total existing IT environment involves a cost. The amount of that cost depends not only on the size and complexity of the initiative being undertaken, but also on the state of the current IT environment.

Think of the experience of companies that had to cope with the year 2000 issue. Some found it simpler to scrap old systems and install new ones rather than to apply the patches and fixes needed to keep their systems running.

However, a forward-looking, cutting-edge project may require that a company upgrade parts of an older system so that the new initiative can reach its full potential. Often, so-called "while we're at it" costs are also involved. Though these costs are technically unnecessary, some feel that it is preferable to absorb them earlier rather than later. In other words, while the IT patient is on the operating table and already opened up, the IT surgeon might be able to save money and time by taking care of a number of issues at once.

Only by analyzing the costs of changes to the existing environment can the *total cost* of an IT initiative truly be captured. However, once the total cost has been dealt with, the budget still needs to accommodate issues surrounding *lifetime cost*. After the IT initiative is bedded down in the company's IT environment, much maintenance cost should not be required in the early years. However, as illustrated in Figure 5.3, over time, maintenance costs increase, geometrically at some point, as the assets age.

This is true not only for applications, but also for hardware, networks, other IT infrastructure items, and services. In fact, maintenance costs are not the only costs that increase. Others include direct and indirect user-related costs, such as down time.

Adding the total cost of an initiative to the lifetime costs of the components involved in the initiative, and doing this for each and every item on the IT budget, helps to define the total IT spend.

CASE STUDY 5.4
Short-Term Planning Leads to Long-Term Disaster

A recently appointed CEO of a business unit in a large electronics manufacturing company decided that implementing a Web-based customer relationship management (CRM) system was crucial to accomplishing the strategic business objectives he had set out to achieve. He established his immediate timetable based on his view of the competitive landscape

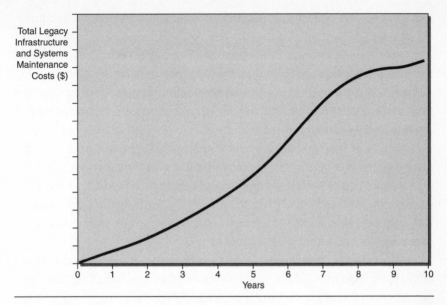

Figure 5.3   Overview of Cost Trends Related to Legacy Infrastructure and Systems.

and his desire to achieve a "quick win" that would position him as the front-running candidate for the corporate CEO job, which would become vacant within a year of the current corporate CEO's retirement.

The company had never before implemented a system that even compared with the contemplated CRM in terms of size, scope, scale, and complexity. Naturally, the IT organization had little experience in dealing with such projects. In addition, the effort would be the company's first major foray into Web-based applications and their related technology infrastructure. But the business-unit CEO had his personal priorities, and the corporate CIO was not about to stand in the way of someone who, within the year, might become his boss.

A project team consisting of IT and business-unit resources was assembled. Team members proceeded to develop the plan for the project. The team had effectively identified one-time development and start-up costs, as well as the planned annual operating and maintenance costs of the system over a period of five years. Although none of its members were completely experienced, the project team developed a reasonably good lifetime analysis of the CRM system's costs.

When the business-unit CEO saw the CRM system cost analysis, he hit the roof. Particularly upsetting was that fact that ongoing maintenance and support costs dwarfed the one-time implementation costs. If he included the total lifetime costs in the ROI calculation, the corporate CEO would never allow the project to go forward.

In spite of the objections of the corporate CIO, the business-unit CEO used only the one-time system implementation costs to calculate a point-in-time ROI instead of one based on the system's lifetime costs. This approach erroneously reflected a *go*-ROI for the project; by providing the corporate CEO with only this point-in-time information, the business-unit CEO received approval to proceed with the project.

Unfortunately, the corporate CIO's role in the company had been in limbo for some time and his relationship with the corporate CEO was tenuous at best. Therefore, he believed he had fulfilled his responsibilities because he had registered his objections with the business-unit CEO who owned the project. He felt he did not need to raise any objections with the corporate CEO. The result of this decision to proceed, which was based on partial information, was a disaster waiting to happen.

What occurred over the next several months was a classic meltdown in IT management. The IT organization, which was relatively inexperienced in CRM systems implementation and Web-based infrastructure, decided that his project would be a great learning experience for the staff. As a result, they decided to "tough it out" and do all of the implementation work in-house, working only with the software vendor on technical issues. The project team was quickly overwhelmed and bogged down; deadlines slipped and costs mounted; and the business-unit CEO became increasingly frustrated, anxious, and aggressive. He implored the CIO to cut corners wherever necessary to get the system up and running.

The originally flawed point-in-time analysis was now even further removed from the lifetime-cost ROI reality. With pressure reaching monumental proportions, the IT organization declared the project successfully completed and launched the new CRM system, problems and all, to meet the arbitrary deadline imposed by the business-unit CIO.

The result was failure, embarrassment, and millions of dollars in write-offs. Both the business-unit CEO and the corporate CIO were shown the door.

Had the true, total lifetime-cost analysis been provided to the corporate CEO, the ROI would never have been adequate to get the project off the ground. Today, several years later, the company is still recovering from the fiasco.

RUTHLESSLY PRIORITIZE DESIRES FOR FUTURE IT

Must have, need to have, and *nice to have* are not the same concepts. If IT is viewed as a free resource by business-unit and corporate departments, every item becomes a must have. Only after certain disciplines are put in place can business units and users move forward and make priority decisions.

During times of transition and in tough economic times or downturns, costs become a particular focus and ruthless prioritization in the IT environment becomes a necessity.

The term *ruthless prioritization* is not intended to be nice. Ruthless prioritization has as its fundamental objective a reduction in the number of IT priorities and total IT spend to levels that a company can afford. Ruthlessly prioritizing focuses business units and users on living within their means and dealing with austerity. It is a form of tough love driven by the CIO.

Once the priorities are sorted out—either to reduce costs or to freeze spending on legacy systems to free up funds to spend on new initiatives— ruthless prioritization must be continued and institutionalized into the regular IT planning process. Only then can anyone be sure that spending on *nice to have* items does not gradually creep back into the budget.

With proper IT planning, budgeting, and spend-portfolio analysis processes in place, ruthless prioritization simply becomes a tactic that helps to infuse the organization's culture with the idea that wise IT spending must be maintained.

CASE STUDY 5.5
Reining in the IT Lone Ranger

A consumer goods company that had been independently owned and operated for many decades had established itself as a premier regional brand in several key U.S. markets. In the 1970s, management sold the company to an investment-oriented portfolio management firm that intended to leverage the brand and accelerate growth of the business, both in the United States and around the world.

After several years, the investment firm sold the company to a global consumer goods production and distribution firm. The new parent company was intent on achieving significant growth but made the mistake of not becoming directly involved in the company management. Instead, it allowed management to revert to managing the company as if it were a stand-alone, private organization with one difference: It was accorded an "unlimited" funding capacity.

A rapid growth strategy and a lack of strong parent company oversight led to numerous accounting abuses that were uncovered after a change in top management. After a special investigation was conducted, the parent company decided to replace the entire management team with executives from corporate headquarters.

IT within the company reported to the CFO. When the new CFO arrived, he attempted to obtain a snapshot of the current status of IT from the CIO, who had not been replaced. After multiple attempts, the new CFO concluded that he was being stonewalled and that the current CIO had something to hide.

The CFO commissioned a special review of the entire IT organization, including IT resources, skills, and capabilities; IT management, budgeting, and control processes; and IT planning and prioritization. The primary objective was to ensure that IT could adequately support the growth strategy that the parent company was planning.

The review uncovered an IT organization that followed no formal IT planning or budgeting process. IT spend was determined almost unilaterally by the CIO and focused primarily on technological matters. The CIO had been responsible for identifying strategic applications needed by the company. His process for doing so involved little or no dialogue with business-unit management. And because outsourcers were hired to implement new applications, the institutional knowledge that might have come from such initiatives was virtually nonexistent.

A baseline IT spend analysis was developed, and a business-oriented planning and budgeting process directly involving business-unit management was created. A complete rejustification and prioritization of current IT spend was performed (both directly with IT and also with the business units) to streamline and concentrate existing IT resources and funds on only the most strategically important areas. A number of nonstrategic projects were canceled, as were a number of contracts with outside vendors and implementation contractors. The new IT budgeting process provided executive management and the business-unit leaders with full transparency of the total IT spend across the entire company. Executives became more involved in setting IT strategy and in planning and budgeting for IT with a focus on ruthless prioritization of competing desires for IT resources.

THE BOTTOM LINE IN BUDGETING

An IT budget will never be perfect, and it will never be static. Unless the company is a start-up and begins with a commitment to totally transparent IT asset management and spending, the CEO, the business–unit leaders, and the CIO will always be in a catch–up mode when trying to develop best practices in total spend analysis and budgeting.

As things change in the business, IT will be forced to stop some projects, start others, or shift its priorities in providing services to particular business–unit departments. This is normal, but the CIO and the IT organization must have the IT budget baseline constructed in such a way that it is fully transparent to corporate and business–unit executives who need to make properly informed decisions.

The CIO's proper role in budgeting is to educate executives and users outside the IT organization about the options they have and about the total costs, benefits, and risks associated with each option. The IT department's finance expert should be crunching the numbers; the CIO should be explaining the significance and business implications of the outcome of that number crunching.

Finally, this budgeting exercise will become easier each year and so will the ability to tease out costs and project future budgets. Over time, the budgeting process will become a more robust exercise that can feed back more useful information into the next round of IT strategy and planning.

The CIO will continuously struggle to identify, aggregate, analyze, and present the IT spend that sits outside the IT organization. However, CEOs should expect and require CIOs to fulfill the responsibility of being ultimately accountable to executive management and to the board regarding IT spend throughout the company. Whether the CIO directly controls all IT spend is not the issue; he or she must be responsible for keeping the spotlight on the total IT spend.

To some, this might be a nontraditional view, but the fact is that the CIO must take on this role to function as a proper member of the executive management team. Acting this way does not necessarily win the CIO many friends, but it does require him or her to play a true executive role.

IT budget makers will improve over time at collecting cost data. They will be able to become more granular in detail. They will gain a better understanding of the company's IT spend and will become better able to explain that spend to users to help them utilize IT resources wisely.

Even without a rigorous accounting system of chargebacks or transfer pricing of services, the IT organization should, over a few years, be 80 to 90 percent of the way there to getting users to understand the consequences of their actions in light of their desires for more and better IT services.

CASE STUDY 5.6

Ruthless Prioritization Transforms IT Spend

When the new CIO came on board at a global information services company, neither a formal budgeting process nor performance metrics existed. Management could not answer the question: How much does the company spend on IT and where do we spend it?

The new CIO inherited a fragmented and generally uncontrolled IT organization comprised of individually run IT units. Gathering the information necessary to achieve a broad-based view of the company, to understanding the total IT spend, or even to categorizing that spend was impossible. Although some IT units had created their own budgets, no organizational IT budget existed, and the individual IT unit budgets employed different definitions and different assumptions.

Because definitions of service levels were not in place, the IT organization was not being held to any defined level of service, and users could easily argue that service was subpar. IT units made unilateral decisions concerning IT expenditures without consulting anyone from the business units. Little effort had been made to aggregate IT procurement among a limited number of vendors to leverage the company's buying power.

Stepping into this situation, the new CIO was determined to establish a meaningful and relevant IT budget over the course of the first year while he was "stabilizing" the IT organization. To do this, he realized that he would have to collect and analyze the data he needed to understand the existing fragmented IT spend across the company.

First, he established an IT chart of accounts that could be used to aggregate and array the data from multiple sources to paint a picture of the main categories of IT spend. The IT chart of accounts was oriented toward management of IT as a full-fledged business unit in the company as opposed to its being a set of financial accounts. In essence, the CIO was setting up an IT-focused, activity-based cost/management accounting database that would allow him to see the categories of IT spend for the various IT assets from a TSA (total spend analysis) perspective.

Data was collected from a variety of sources. Some were taken directly from the company's accounting, payroll, HR, accounts payable, billing, and other core systems. These were disaggregated and reconstructed to provide information specific to IT. Other data had to be retrieved and entered manually. The process was time consuming and tedious, but after several months, the CIO felt he had captured a picture of the company's IT spend that was 70 to 80 percent complete. This was enough for him to see some prominent trends, to draw some important conclusions, and to make some key decisions.

The following are some of the major trends and conclusions drawn from this analysis:

- Procurement of PCs, software, servers, and specialized services was performed locally, with different vendors in each location. This required the expenditure of enormous amounts of IT staff time in each location and highlighted the need to drive volume purchase/discount arrangements with a select group of key vendors.
- Ninety-five percent of the overall IT spend was focused on maintaining aging and already-obsolete IT infrastructure and applications (both PC- and mainframe-based). At the same time, virtually no funding was available for strategic initiatives designed to reduce the IT organization's long-term costs and to improve the value and service it provided.

- A huge amount of primary asset duplication existed across the company. More than 600 servers were spread over the office locations, and most were less than 30 percent utilized. In addition, even with all of the excess capacity, no attempt was made to use this available resource to provide a backup and recovery/redundancy buffer. (When one server utilized at 30 percent of capacity went down, a means could not be found to switch over to several similar, less utilized servers situated right next to it.)
- IT staffing and skills patterns and associated compensation and development costs were all over the map, depending on which office one looked at. Also absent was any ability to assess the entire complement of IT skills across the company as a single resource pool with any critical mass.

As a result of reconstructing the then-current IT budget, the CIO was able to identify major pockets of inefficiency, redundancy, duplicative spend, and critical unfunded needs. To begin correcting this situation in the short term and knowing that he would not be receiving any additional funding during the first year, the CIO placed a moratorium on all outstanding noncritical, nonemergency legacy IT infrastructure and systems requests.

At the time, of more than 800 such outstanding requests, none had been organized into any order of priority. Using a ruthless prioritization process, the CIO forced all users to rejustify their requests, which were then organized into four priority categories having the following characteristics:

1. Ongoing infrastructure or production support
   — To restore infrastructure/production environment
   — Requires immediate attention
   — Given top priority—no priority discussion required.
2. Mandatory requests
   — To comply with legal requirements—scheduled to avoid noncompliance and subsequent penalties
   — Receive very high priority for scheduling
   — Have little or no flexibility in terms of implementation date.
3. Prioritized requests
   — Require business-unit sponsorship and review
   — Require assessment of business value, speed, and effort; based on implementation rationale

— Require estimate of costs and benefits
— Given final priority as jointly determined by IT and the business unit (conflicts and competing requests resolved)
— Scheduled on the basis of available resources.
4. Strategic requests
— Funded on the basis of long-term strategic objectives and as part of the overall IT planning process
— Include new foundation infrastructure and systems
— Include other strategic needs.

Each request was then given a rating based on four sets of criteria:

1. Business value rating
2. Speed rating (elapsed time from start to finish)
3. Ease of accomplishment rating (IT and user hours)
4. Costs and benefits rating.

The criteria for each rating are illustrated in Table 5.2.

This prioritization process reduced the number of outstanding requests from 800 to the 30 that really mattered and that were most critical and reduced the spend on legacy infrastructure and systems from 90 percent to about 50 percent. This, in turn, freed up 40 percent of the budget to use on other, more strategic initiatives during the first year, including new foundation IT infrastructure and system efforts that could have a profound effect on strategically reducing the total IT spend.

Once this ruthless prioritization process was completed, the CIO began building a proper IT budget process and, over the first year of the transition, developed an IT budget with four primary spend categories:

1. Ongoing legacy infrastructure and system maintenance and production
2. Legacy infrastructure and system enhancement
3. New foundation infrastructure and systems
4. Other strategic initiatives.

The newly available funds were shifted to a variety of foundation infrastructure and system efforts, including a number easily identified as IT-specific items and a number of items about which the business units could agree. This shift in IT spending is illustrated in Figure 5.4 on page 149.

Table 5.2   Example of Prioritization Criteria

Business Value Rating
Very high: Mandatory legal/compliance requirements
High: Direct linkage to strategic company/business-unit initiatives
Medium: Direct linkage to tactical company/business initiative
Low: Efficiency, convenience, minimal company/business impact.

Speed Rating (Elapsed Time from Start to Finish)
Very high: Can be completed in one month or less
High: Can be completed in two months or less
Medium: Can be completed in three months or less
Low: Requires more than three months to complete.

Ease of Accomplishment Rating (IT and User Hours)
Very high: Up to 80 hours
High: 81–160 hours
Medium: 161–1,000 hours
Low: More than 1,000 hours.

Costs and Benefits Statement
Total cost analysis
Timing of benefits.

The first year's impact was dramatic. In addition, as projects moved forward into the second year, a more formalized IT budgeting process was established that involved the development of a core IT services list, a service gap analysis, determination of standard and premium service requirements by business units, identification of IT costs residing in the business units, and a continuing dialogue among them concerning the drivers of these costs. In addition, the first IT SLAs were prepared and tested, and an automated IT budget model was developed for use across the company.

WHAT THE CEO CAN DO TO ENSURE THAT IT SPEND IS TRANSPARENT TO ALL PARTIES

Getting to the bottom of the total real IT spend and fully understanding it is often a grueling, time-consuming, and relentless activity. However, establishing the proper baseline of IT spend and of the IT budgeting process

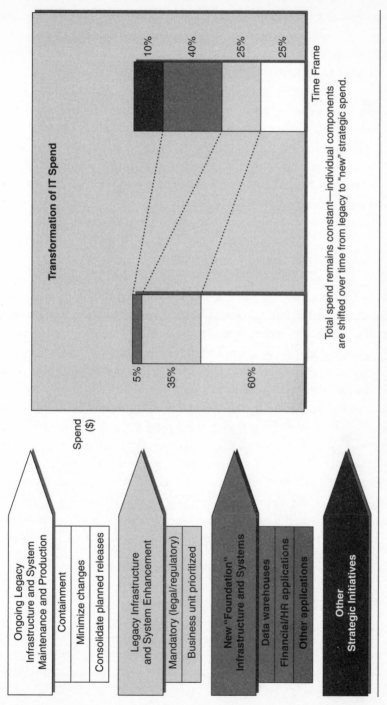

Figure 5.4 IT Spend Shift.

and incorporating costs in the IT organization and those in the business units are the most important first steps toward managing IT as a business.

CEOs can take five concrete steps to ensure that the total real IT spend is transparent to all parties. The CEO should:

1. Make sure that everyone on the executive management team fully understands the key drivers of IT spend, whether these costs reside in the IT organization or in the business units. In addition, the CEO should ensure that specific ownership responsibility and accountability are clearly defined for all parties (IT, business units, corporate departments, and users) and appropriately measured.

2. Stress the importance to everyone on the executive management team of evaluating IT expenditures using the total IT spend across the company and not just point-in-time spend in the IT organization.

3. Ensure that all business–unit leaders approach the IT budgeting process from the standpoint of *value for money* and that they fully understand the direct correlation between IT spend and service levels, their ownership of the key drivers, and the ability they have to affect these service levels and costs as a result of that ownership.

4. Decide if a *ruthless prioritization* effort is needed for IT spend at the company to move that spend to a zero base. The CEO should focus attention on transforming the IT spend in the company by shifting funds focused on maintaining legacy infrastructure and systems to investments in new *foundation* IT infrastructure and systems.

5. Ensure that the CIO is competent to perform the complex, multidimensional task of IT budgeting and negotiating across multiple constituencies in the company. The CEO should determine if the CIO needs help in the IT budgeting and spend analysis areas and, if so, provide direct assistance and an appropriate level of financial or professional support.

CHAPTER 6

Focus on Outcomes, Not Process

Using Metrics to Enhance IT Credibility

The new CIO of a global information services company inherited not only a fragmented IT organization with no consistent budgeting, but also an organization that had virtually no performance metrics.

At the same time that the IT spend database was being assembled, the CIO commissioned a comprehensive review to identify and determine the key IT performance metrics that needed to be in place for staff to be able to manage all aspects of the IT organization going forward. He was looking to begin the process of moving the IT organization toward a performance-based culture that recognized accountability as a key principle.

In doing so, the CIO wanted to ensure that all performance measurement was executed on a root-cause basis, that is, that the objective of the performance analysis was to identify patterns or trends among problems in advance so corrective action could be taken before they became unmanageable. A common performance-reporting format was established for everyone in the IT organization to use for any type of metric (e.g., IT value measurements, general IT measures, operational measures, procurement and sourcing measures, help desk measures).

Implementing a common approach to IT performance measurement and reporting enabled anyone in the IT organization easily to move to another role and to understand the process used in measuring and managing performance. The IT performance measurement reports focused on point-in-time and trend data, operational and financial statistics, root causes, and corrective actions.

The CIO's objective was not to inundate everyone with a large volume of metrics but, rather, to identify the few most relevant ones. To accomplish this, the CIO set out two categories of IT metrics—static and dynamic—recognizing that the performance measurements used would change over time as the IT organization evolved. Dynamic metrics were those appropriate to use during times of change and transition; static metrics were those to be used during steady-state operations.

For example, certain types of project and conversion metrics were dynamic, as were metrics surrounding one-time special activities. Dynamic metrics were particularly useful during the restructuring period. Once certain functions within the IT organization reached a steady state, static metrics were used to measure and continually enhance performance. The most common static metrics are service levels, run rates, available time, turnover rate, and so on.

In addition, the CIO established formal roles in the organization that had specific responsibilities in the IT performance measurement process. These roles had not existed previously. Within a period of several months, IT performance measurement had become a regular and accepted part of the new high-performance, high-quality IT culture the CIO was looking to establish.

People knew that if the metrics for which they were accountable were not trending in the right direction, they had responsibility to seek help from others in the IT organization to correct problems and to bring the metrics back in line. The compensation and reward systems reinforced this behavior. Everyone in the IT organization learned that the primary responsibility of the metrics was improvement and prevention, rather than punishment.

The credibility of the IT organization and the CIO was greatly enhanced when the CIO began publishing quarterly reports showing the entire company how the IT organization measured up against its goals and against outside benchmarks on a host of both static and dynamic metrics. The CIO clearly stated that he and the IT organization agreed to be held accountable for making its targets not only in delivering projects on time and on budget, but also in delivering ongoing services at the agreed-on quality and service levels. The IT organization was now functioning like any other customer-facing business unit in the company, and the IT people were being viewed more and more as responsible and accountable professionals, rather than simply as technical support staff.

An industry study of 26 companies in the late 1990s[1] found that 58 percent of CIOs were measured on and held accountable for project performance, 50 percent for infrastructure availability, and 50 percent for staying within the appropriated budget. However, only 25 percent of CIOs were measured on how satisfied user *customers* were with the *product* being provided by the IT organization. Only 8 percent were held accountable for compliance with standards and only 8 percent for meeting personnel retention goals.

The survey also found that dissatisfaction with IT performance against these metrics was not often met with attempts to correct root-cause problems. Rather, it was met with attempts to cut the IT budget or limit its growth relative to other budgets in the company.

In too many companies, IT metrics focus on operational, technical, and transactional components, such as up time, programming productivity, and help desk response times and on whether projects are on time and on budget. Unfortunately, these shop-floor type metrics alone do not get at the heart of what the executive team needs to know about the IT organization, namely, how effectively the IT organization is positioning itself to be used by its constituents as a driver of business value.

Sometimes, these operational metrics may look good but are actually masking problems. For instance, if an IT organization representative says, "Look how productive our help desk is; we answered 1,200 calls this month," he or she may be masking the fact that user training on new software has been haphazard or that substandard quality equipment has been purchased. If training were better, the help desk volume might be cut in half, and better quality control with new PCs might significantly reduce the number of break/fix maintenance calls.

IT metrics need to be value focused, performance based, and improvement oriented—not only production based. The metrics must help to identify root causes and to drive specific actions and behaviors within the IT

---

[1] U.K. Government IT Survey, PricewaterhouseCoopers (1997).

organization and positive, cooperative remediation efforts between IT and the business units.

As noted by Lewis Clark, Principal Analyst, IT Services Performance Metrics for Gartner:

> IT performance measurement and assessment is a discipline that requires well-honed practices of gathering metrics and applying them to meet specific objectives, including:
>
> - Recognizing and emulating industry-leading levels of performance
> - Evaluating different functional areas within the IS organization in order to identify strengths and improve upon weaknesses
> - Keeping a firm grasp on the business during lean times or periods of market volatility
> - Preparing for a shift from cost-containment to revenue-generation priorities.
>
> Organizations need to monitor a whole array of factors that affect financial and operational performance. Even for benchmarks that are in common use, there can be a wide range of optimal values for different types of businesses or functions. Managers need to understand the enterprise's performance relative to its own history and immediate peer group (rather than the market at large). Given solid data and a clear understanding of causes and effects, they can take any necessary preventative or corrective actions.[2]

A PHILOSOPHY OF MEASUREMENT

The only reason to spend time and money collecting and analyzing performance data and disseminating measurement results is to enable individuals to identify and act on trends, catch problems before they become insurmountable, and prevent little problems from becoming catastrophic. Proper use of performance metrics results in changes needed to create desired outcomes.

An IT organization needs one set of metrics to measure its internal performance and other sets of metrics to measure its relationships with business units and with the corporation and its overall value to the business.

---

[2] Lewis Clark, "Applying Performance Metrics and Benchmarking to the IT Services Organization (Executive Summary)," *Gartner Dataquest* (June 6, 2002): 1.

Metrics should not be used as a whip by managers who want to punish subordinates or by a business unit or corporate executives who want to punish the IT organization. Metrics should be used as the basis for factual and ongoing dialogue about how to improve performance. Focusing on outcomes, not on the measurement process itself, is what's most important.

The data used for measuring must be credible, verifiable, and transparent. All parties affected by the metric must have confidence in the quality of the data being analyzed. And all parties who will use the metric must agree to the rules governing analysis of the data. In addition, the way the analysis and reporting is approached by anyone performing the measurement must be consistent.

Accountability and responsibility for using metrics for corrective action should always be placed at a point closest to the action taking place.

CASE STUDY 6.2
Confusing Process with Purpose

A large, multidivision manufacturing and distribution company in the medical supply industry prided itself on its performance measurement systems. The company had been founded by a group of engineers who had developed some unique manufacturing technologies and processes that enabled them to produce and distribute their products at a cost considerably below that borne by the rest of the market.

At the core of the company's success stood a very detailed and robust performance measurement system that focused on manufacturing, distribution, and customer management. The company measured and compared product and customer-facing matters very precisely. But this was not the case with the company's internal operating functions (i.e., finance, accounting, human resources, and IT). All of these areas were considered support functions and were relegated to second-class treatment by a product- and customer-focused executive management team.

As the company moved through its start-up and early growth phases, these internal functions worked well enough and adequately supported the company. However, as the organization grew, both organically and through acquisitions, and as new executives were brought in from the outside to oversee the incremental growth and the demands being placed on these internal functions, it became very apparent that unless some professional discipline were applied, including rigorous performance measurement, chaos would result.

Although some rudimentary operating measures were in place in the organization, no formal or structured measurement program existed across the board. The company had, for the first time, hired a CIO from the outside to replace the manager who had run IT for many years.

Because the CIO had a strong engineering background and had grown up in an IT operations environment, his profile tracked well with the company's executive leadership. One of the first things he was asked to accomplish was the implementation of a "proper" performance measurement system in the IT organization.

The CIO went to work aggressively, trying to make this happen. However, because his background was in operations, he focused almost exclusively on operational measurements (i.e., the IT physical plant). His detailed and precise nature ensured that virtually every piece of data was collected, combined, calculated, compared, analyzed, and stored. Before long, his bookshelf contained huge binders filled with every possible IT operational measure anyone could ever ask for.

He required his top IT managers to sift through and review all measurement data and to prepare lengthy reports on all that was measured. Weekly, biweekly, and monthly meetings (some of which lasted for days) were held to "discuss the numbers." The CIO was very proud of the performance measurement process he had developed and implemented, and, on the surface, the company's executives seemed pleased because performance measurement was important to them.

However, in the real world of the IT organization, all was not well. Burdened and weary, the IT managers and staff were tiring of the process. In fact, the IT performance measurement process really had no impact on day-to-day operations. Reams of data and reports were produced, but nothing was really done to turn the data into actionable information. The process of data collection and performance measurement had overtaken the purpose of performance measurement—to identify trends early on and to drive specific improvements.

People in the IT organization became demoralized and many began to leave. Ironically, the very performance- and measurement-oriented CIO actually had no organizational performance measures in place to help him understand turnover trends and other human resource issues. All he had was anecdotal information about why some IT people were leaving. Over time, the IT organization became depleted of key skills, and the burden of the IT performance measurement colossus the CIO had built fell to the remaining employees, who became more and more demoralized and less and less productive.

After some time, the company's executive management realized that although the CIO was producing many nice-looking performance reports, the company was not getting what it really needed out of the IT organization in the way of service. The CIO—and, for that matter, the entire IT organization—had lost its way and could not see the forest any longer because of the focus on so many trees.

Ultimately, both the CIO and his performance measurement colossus were scrapped as the first step in restructuring the company's IT organization. After some discussion, the CEO initiated direct discussions with a number of IT outsourcing providers to operate the company's IT environment.

MEASURING THE BUSINESS VALUE OF IT

To link IT performance to corporate performance, IT metrics must measure and communicate IT performance in the context of the business value IT provides. IT operational performance cannot be considered in a vacuum. All metrics should "roll up" to answer three key questions for C-level executives:

1. How is IT spending the company's money?
2. Is the company receiving the agreed-on value for its IT spending?
3. Is IT helping the company to meet its strategic and tactical goals and objectives?

The manner in which IT metrics are implemented and acted on is what differentiates successful measurement programs from those that fail. Successful measures are:

- Relevant
- Practical

- Actionable
- Reported or communicated
- Owned.

Successful Measures Are Relevant

Metrics need to be relevant to what is being measured. They need to be tied to a specific goal or objective and to measure elements that are key to success. Metrics that are relevant to the IT organization are not necessarily relevant to business-unit managers or to other consumers of IT services.

For example, an IT operational performance metric focusing on the frequency of specific problems handled by the help desk would have considerable relevance to the help desk functional manager and, possibly, even to the business-unit IT liaison. However, the business-unit leaders, the CEO, the CFO, and other executives would probably not find this metric to be of much relevance or value in their areas of focus.

Successful Measures Are Practical

Too many metrics for any one task, activity, or role dilute people's ability to use them to solve problems and to change behavior. Research indicates that three-to-five highly focused metrics are usually the right amount; more overwhelm the individuals being measured.

I am reminded here of the new CIO, who, in her zeal to measure IT performance, created a set of hundreds of metrics that could fill a telephone book. Her concept was correct, but her execution was highly impractical. The process of preparing these metrics for her on a monthly basis required a full week and literally stopped most of the IT functions dead in their tracks. In addition, once she received all of the metrics reports, she then spent another week analyzing all the data. The result was a lot of motion but very little action to improve performance.

Successful Measures Are Actionable

For a metric to be useful, an individual must be able to use the metric to direct and guide future actions. Individuals, activities, and functions must be measured in such a way that the people responsible for what is being measured can take concrete actions to change or correct the performance that is being measured.

For example, if the person responsible for the company's networks sees a pattern of continuing decay or backup in telecommunications services, he or she should be able to intervene immediately and directly with the telecommunications service provider(s) to ensure that service is restored to acceptable levels. Because the network leader personally owns the telecommunications service metrics and is empowered to take actions to keep the metric in line, he or she is able rapidly to control or correct a potentially disastrous situation.

Successful Measures Are Reported or Communicated

A metric that goes unreported is like a tree falling in an empty forest. Reporting and communicating metrics to everyone in the organization makes those metrics real. They must be reported to different constituencies in different ways that explain and validate the relevance of the metric to that constituency.

I have known a number of CIOs who believe that if they selectively report only the metrics that make IT look good, their performance will be viewed very positively. However, in several of these cases, I have also seen business-unit users put in place their own "shadow IT metrics" because they do not trust what the CIO is reporting. By not communicating the IT performance data and metrics in a transparent manner, the CIO is playing a spin game and creating a credibility gap, thereby reducing his or her ability to identify root causes and to aggressively resolve problem areas.

Successful Measures Are Owned

When an individual or team owns a metric, that person or group is accountable for performing up to the appropriate level at which that metric is positive. Without accountability for improvement against a particular target, no improvement will occur.

Well-designed IT metrics can help teach technical people in the IT organization to make decisions in a businesslike way. If an individual owns the metric, he or she also decides how to use it to change future outcomes and, in turn, is responsible for the result of that decision making. The same applies to IT management and control and to IT business value metrics in which executives outside the IT organization might have an interest.

In one IT organization, the CIO did a very effective job of getting the business units to take ownership of the metrics associated with PC spend by jointly (IT and business unit) establishing a head count-driven, standard class of user approach to the acquisition, deployment, and support of PCs throughout the company. Using this approach enabled the business units to own the PC total cost metric (i.e., if the business unit's head count increased, so did the total number of PCs and the total cost for PCs; also, if the class of use requirements increased because of changing user needs, so did the total cost for PCs). The CIO and the IT organization owned the per-unit cost metric for PCs (i.e., they were responsible for driving down the individual cost for all classes of PC by driving volume deals with the vendors and establishing more cost-efficient configurations). With such metrics ownership clearly defined and agreed on upfront, the entire PC acquisition, deployment, and support process, and its resulting costs, were owned and everyone involved worked in a streamlined and collaborative manner.

DIFFERENT METRICS FOR DIFFERENT AUDIENCES

Figure 6.1 illustrates how the universe of metrics is divided in such a way that the right audiences see the metrics and how taking corrective action is driven to the proper level.

Because many people play a number of different roles, they will receive different sets of metrics for different reasons. For instance, everyone is a computer user, so everyone has some desire and reason to see operational performance metrics. But operational performance metrics do not need to be part of the package of metrics delivered to C-level executives in their role as executives. These individuals need to be basing business decisions on a different set of metrics—those that speak to the issue of IT business value.

In the remainder of this chapter, I focus on IT business value metrics—how they can be constructed, what they tell corporate and business-unit leadership about how well they are using IT to derive business value, and how well they are operating IT as a business.

IT business value metrics need to reflect the key drivers of the IT organization. However, to do that effectively, the IT organization must have some sort of uniform structural *IT management lens,* such as the one illustrated in Figure 6.2 on page 162. Such a view ensures an appropriate level of consistency by which the IT business value metrics are assessed.

IT business value metrics can be defined across each of six critical drivers—alignment, support, operations, resiliency, leverage, and futures—

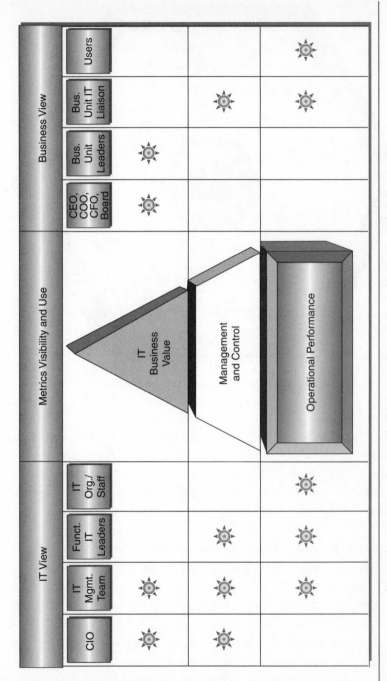

Figure 6.1 IT Metrics Overview.

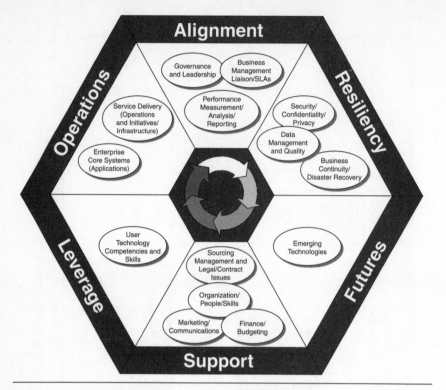

Figure 6.2   IT Management Lens.

described in the book's introduction. In addition, for each IT business value metric, users must be able to determine where in the company its use is most applicable—for example, is the metric applicable across the enterprise or only within specific business units or functional areas? The following are some guidelines:

- Enterprisewide IT business value metrics are typically those that have broadest possible applicability across all parts of the company, either at the corporate or a business-unit level. Such metrics are generally high level and independent of the specifics of a business unit or functional area.

  An example of an enterprisewide IT business value metric is the growth rate of total IT employees per growth rate of total company employees described as a ratio (e.g., a slower IT employee growth rate in relation to the overall corporatewide employee growth rate would illustrate that the IT organization is doing a good job in leveraging its existing capacity).

- Business-unit-specific IT business value metrics are typically metrics that are relevant only to specific business units. These metrics are typically somewhat more detailed than the enterprisewide metrics and address IT issues associated with revenue-producing parts of the company.

  An example of a business-unit-specific IT business value metric is the attributable IT spend related to that business unit per number of direct employees in the business unit (e.g., an increasing trend in the IT spend per employee would illustrate that the IT organization is not doing as effective a job as possible in taking advantage of IT economies of scale).

- Functional area-specific IT business value metrics are similar to business-unit-specific metrics in that they are relevant only to a specific department in the company. In this case, the IT business value metrics are focused on the business's non-revenue-producing/support functions. An example of a functional area-specific IT business value metric is the growth rate of attributable IT spend per growth rate of direct total functional department spend (e.g., an increasing trend in IT spend compared with functional departmental spend would suggest that IT spend is not being very effective in leveraging its current capabilities and in absorbing business growth).

The reality is that the *right* IT metrics are neither the same nor relevant for every organization. I once worked with a CIO who tried desperately to emulate another very successful CIO by setting up an IT measurement system that was very similar to the one the first CIO had implemented. The system even included the same metrics. The only problem was that many of these metrics did not really apply to the second CIO's company (they were in different industries). The good news was that the second CIO quickly realized his error, regrouped, and changed the IT metrics with which he started to metrics that made more sense for his company. Table 6.1 provides a framework for identifying where the different types of IT business value metrics are most appropriately applied.

Table 6.1   Applicability and Use of IT Business Value Metrics[a]

IT Business Value Areas/Metrics	Applicability and Use		
	Enterprisewide	Business Unit Specific	Functional Area Specific
Alignment • Attributable IT spend[b] per direct employee[c] (budget, actual).		✓	
Support • Growth rate of total IT employees per growth rate of total employees (budget, actual).	✓		
Operations • Growth rate of attributable IT spend per growth rate of direct total spend (cost) (budget, actual).			✓
Resiliency • •			
Leverage • •			
Futures • •			

[a] Example for illustrative purposes.
[b] Attributable IT spend = Total IT spend allocable to that part of the business.
[c] Direct employees = Employees directly involved in that specific part of the business.

DIFFERENT METRICS FOR DIFFERENT CATEGORIES OF IT INVESTMENTS

Understanding how IT provides business value requires dividing the universe of IT investments (IT assets) into four broad categories. Each category has a set of business value characteristics, a typical set of business value outcomes, and a few key metrics that can be established to determine if the outcomes are being achieved.

As Figure 6.3 illustrates, the four categories of IT investments can be graphically depicted as a pyramid and are, from the base of the pyramid to

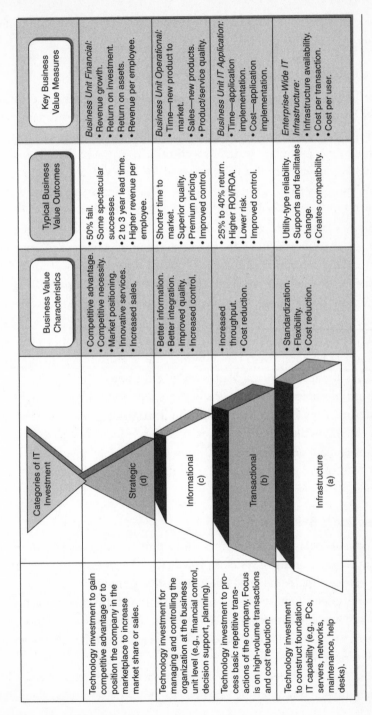

Figure 6.3 Business Value Measures for IT.

the top, infrastructure, transactional systems, informational systems, and strategic information systems.

Infrastructure

Infrastructure is the foundation of IT capability. It is delivered as reliable services shared throughout the company and should be coordinated centrally by the IT organization. Investments in infrastructure are large and often long term (although utility aspects of infrastructure investment such as network connectivity can be contracted for on a shorter term basis).

The business value characteristics of infrastructure are derived from its ability quickly and economically to enable the implementation of new technology solutions, often across business units. These, in turn, generate economies or value and allow for standardization of services—for example, one integrated telecommunications network or uniform customer database. Standards allow for compatibility of systems across business units and for cost reduction through volume purchasing of hardware, software, and downstream service and maintenance.

Outcomes of a well-run IT infrastructure include a utility-type level of reliability: The user turns the system on and it runs, it is available 24/7, complaints about service are dealt with quickly, and so on.

IT infrastructure metrics are enterprisewide and focus on IT infrastructure. They include availability (up time), cost per transaction, and cost per user. As illustrated in Figure 6.3 (the "a" block of the pyramid), major investment and management issues about IT infrastructure are very similar to those that apply to managing the public infrastructure of roads and bridges.

Transactional Systems

Transactional systems are sometimes referred to as *management control systems*. Investments in these systems provide the IT capabilities necessary for users to process the company's basic, repetitive transactions.

These systems (enterprise resource planning [ERP] software is perhaps the best-known current example) are designed to cut transaction-processing costs by substituting capital for labor or to enable users to handle higher volumes of transactions.

Value from increased investment in transactional systems is embedded in streamlining and integrating processes to increase transaction *throughput* and cut costs, thus improving companywide return on assets (ROA) and return on investment (ROI).

In addition to improving control, such systems reduce risk by reducing the number of manual interventions and touch points and by standardizing the key processes. This, in turn, reduces the potential for multiple interpretations and improves overall data quality and reliability. The net result is better, more stable data and more reliable information, which effectively reduce the risks associated with processing large volumes of transactions. As illustrated in Figure 6.3 (the "b" block of the pyramid), transactional metrics focus on IT applications at the business–unit level and involve the time and cost of application implementation.

Informational Systems

Informational systems are used for managing and controlling the organization at the business–unit level. Systems in this category support management and financial controls as well as decisions.

Information has little value in and of itself. The application of information to decisions leads to business value. Information systems are effective in improving operational performance when they are used for decision support at the business–unit level.

Data warehouses and customer relationship management (CRM) and decision support/analysis software are examples of informational systems. These systems improve the information available to decision makers, which improves integration, quality, and overall control and can allow the company to reduce time to market, improve product quality, and command premium pricing.

Value metrics are operational in nature and focus on the business unit. As illustrated in Figure 6.3 (the "c" block of the pyramid), they include measures of time to market, product and service quality, and sales.

Strategic Information Systems

Strategic information systems are designed to increase competitive advantage or to position the company in the marketplace to increase market share or sales. These systems are usually new for an industry at a particular time and, therefore, are inherently risky and potentially disruptive to the competitive environment.

Examples of strategic information systems that have changed the competitive face of business are automated teller machines (ATMs) and Internet retailing. These types of systems allow for faster time to market, or they allow the company to charge a premium price. They are also perceived as providing superior quality or convenience and often generate higher revenues per employee.

Implementing these systems is also risky. Approximately 50 percent of these efforts fail, and even those that are spectacularly successful often take two to three years to fully implement.

Metrics for strategic systems are financial in nature, focusing on revenue growth, ROA, ROI, and revenue per employee. As illustrated in Figure 6.3 (the "d" block of the pyramid), these systems are oriented toward the business unit.

Without question, different metrics must be applied to the four different categories of IT investment. I worked with the IT organization of a well-managed company in the high-end consumer products industry that did not do a very good job of segregating these different types of investments. In fact, they were attempting to apply the same metrics in the same way across all categories. This muddied the waters and created a skewed view of the true performance of the company's IT investment portfolio.

THE CIO DASHBOARD

The CIO should have available a real-time picture of 12 to 20 of the most important IT organization macro metrics. Some of these should be project-oriented metrics that tie to the hot spots on which IT is working at any time. These metrics should be refreshed and changed as project life cycles ebb and flow. Others should be ongoing static metrics that measure IT operations.

Friction occurs at the point where activities, operations, functions, disciplines, departments, or business units interact. Metrics should be placed at these touch points to measure the amount of friction that occurs.

Figure 6.4 illustrates how the CIO dashboard should be organized around the IT management lens.

Typically, a CIO dashboard one-pager, organized according to the six IT management lens drivers and 14 competency areas, would sit on top of a variety of more detailed level two screens that each focus on individual metrics.

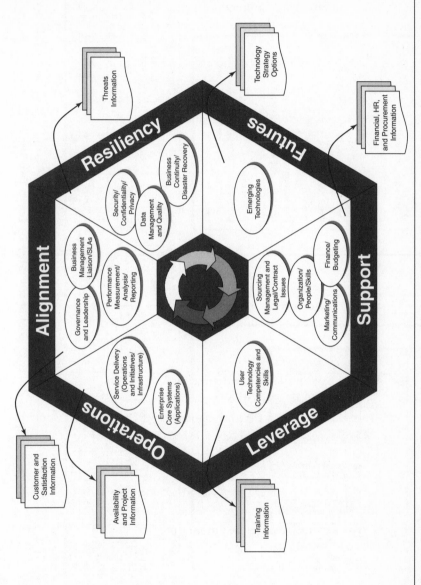

Figure 6.4 CIO Dashboard.

Commentary

What was planned?
Reduction in spend on new capability was desired.

What happened?
Spend increased by 1% over prior year.

Root cause:
Unplanned M&A activity.

Consequences:
Business unit involved in M&A activity must cover incremental IT spend.

Action plan:
Determine potential future issues for subsequent year during annual review cycle.

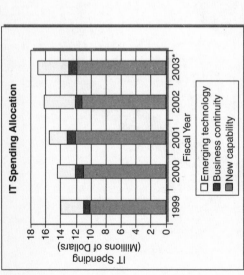

IT Spending Allocation

	Actual Spending ($)			IT Spending Allocation ($)			IT Spending Allocation (Percentage)		
Year	CapEx	OpEx	Total IT Spending ($)	New Capability	Business Continuity	Emerging Technology	New Capability	Business Continuity	Emerging Technology
1999	750,000	13,294,416	14,044,416	10,000,000	1,000,000	3,044,416	71	7.1	21.7
2000	787,500	13,959,137	14,746,637	11,000,000	1,010,000	2,736,637	75	6.8	18.6
2001	826,875	14,657,094	15,483,969	12,000,000	1,020,100	2,463,869	77	6.6	15.9
2002	868,219	15,389,948	16,258,167	11,050,000	1,030,301	4,177,866	68	6.3	25.7
2003*	911,630	16,159,446	17,071,075	11,750,000	1,050,000	4,271,075	69	6.2	25.0

* YTD actual number plus projected budget number for the remaining year.
Note: Example for illustrative purposes.

Figure 6.5 CIO Dashboard: Metrics Level-Two Page.

Figure 6.5 illustrates what a typical CIO dashboard level-two screen might look like for the particular metric, *IT spending allocation*. (The statistical information in Figure 6.5 is for the purpose of illustration and does not imply appropriate or inappropriate levels.)

CASE STUDY 6.3

Using Metrics to Enhance Procurement

A new CIO in a global company with a large staff of customer service employees quickly realized that driving standardization into the company would be one key aspect of accomplishing downstream efficiencies and cost savings in the IT organization and service improvements for users throughout the company.

The first step was to convince the user population and the IT staff that the majority of people in the company had very similar needs when it came to PCs, software, and service. All of the variations in needs could realistically be consolidated into three or four "classes of use." Instead of configuring each PC individually as it was purchased, an agreement could be developed to purchase PCs configured to meet the needs of one of the particular classes of users.

Once appropriate class-of-use policies had been established, a standard image and configuration was developed and agreed to by all business units and corporate departments. The standard image would be placed on every PC; anything other than or beyond the standard image would be considered business unit specific. This was important for defining both the costs to be incurred by the business unit for procurement and the metrics. For instance, if a business unit had a unique image or images but wanted to pay only the standard cost for a help desk, it would have to accept a lower service level against the help-desk metrics.

Other decisions were made about the procurement program: It would be managed by an outside party that would obtain computers from a number of vendors to provide the number needed by the company, do the configuration, burn the standard image (or business unit-specific image), and deliver the PCs where necessary.

The PCs were on a two-year lease cycle, and, after swapping out new machines for any that were clearly obsolete, the company settled into a steady drumbeat of rotating new machines to about one-eighth of the workforce each calendar quarter. (This meant that a few people had to hold on to their first new machines for up to two and a half years to even the flow.)

The company developed a true partnership relationship with the procurement outsourcer. Management worked with the third-party provider to define the process flow (illustrated in Figure 6.6) and the metrics (marked in letters along the flow in Figure 6.6 and described in detail in Figure 6.7 on page 174).

Although the process flow itself might appear complicated on the surface, it actually simplified and clarified all aspects of the entire relationship with the third party. Some of the key principles embodied in and highlighted by the process flow and accompanying metrics description include:

- Establishing and maintaining key relationships at the top executive levels
- Applying account management and partnering concepts
- Focusing on long-term, win-win scenarios instead of short-term, vendor/contract, price-only approaches
- Using a total spend analysis approach to ensure that the full impact of every decision is explored and understood
- Embedding integrated performance metrics across the key processes
- Using performance metrics for purposes of learning and improvement, rather than just to punish one group or another
- Focusing constantly on improvements in total spend and service levels
- Encouraging an open, fully coordinated environment with shared information, balance, and flexibility.

Dynamic (Transition) versus Static (Steady-State Service) Metrics

One-size IT metrics do not fit all IT environments. Different types of metrics are used in different situations. One of the most profound mistakes made in implementing IT performance metrics occurs when people apply static metrics (those used to measure steady-state service levels) in an environment that is undergoing massive change and transition. In times of change, static measures and dynamic measures should be used where appropriate.

For those parts of the IT organization that will continue to operate in a business-as-usual mode even during periods of broader change and transition,

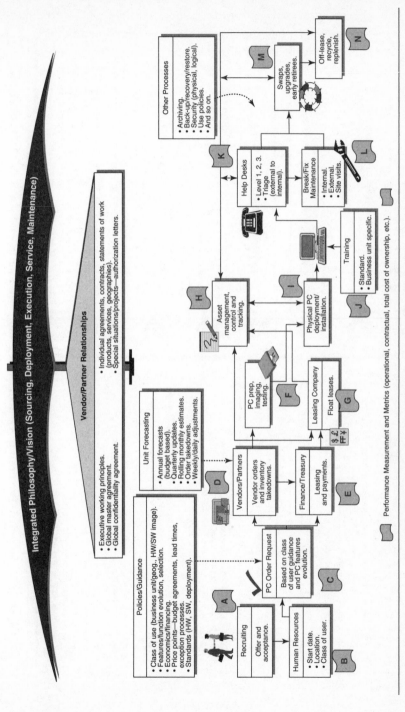

Integrated Philosophy/Vision (Sourcing, Deployment, Execution, Service, Maintenance)

Vendor/Partner Relationships
- Executive working principles.
- Global master agreement.
- Global confidentiality agreement.

- Individual agreements, contracts, statements of work (products, services, geographies).
- Special situations/projects—authorization letters.

Policies/Guidance
- Class of use (business unit/geog., HW/SW image).
- Features/function evolution, selection.
- Economics/financing.
- Price points—budget agreements, lead times, exception processes.
- Standards (HW, SW, deployment).

Unit Forecasting
- Annual forecasts (budget based).
- Quarterly updates.
- Rolling monthly estimates.
- Order takedowns.
- Weekly/daily adjustments.

Recruiting
- Offer and acceptance.

Human Resources
- Start date.
- Location.
- Class of user.

PC Order Request
- Based on class of user guidance and PC features evolution.

Vendors/Partners
- Vendor orders and inventory takedowns.

Finance/Treasury
- Leasing and payments.

PC prep, imaging, testing.

Leasing Company
- Float leases.

Asset management, control and tracking.

Physical PC deployment/installation.

Training
- Standard.
- Business unit specific.

Help Desks
- Level 1, 2, 3.
- Triage (external to internal).

Break/Fix Maintenance
- Internal.
- External.
- Site visits.

Other Processes
- Archiving.
- Back-up/recovery/restore.
- Security (physical, logical).
- Use policies.
- And so on.

Swaps, upgrades, early retirees.

Off-lease, recycle, replenish.

A B C D E F G H I J K L M N

Performance Measurement and Metrics (operational, contractual, total cost of ownership, etc.).

Figure 6.6 Sourcing/Partnering: Overall Flow Example—Total Spend Analysis (TSA)/Metrics.

173

Description of Key Metrics

A
- Timeliness of recruiting/hiring forecasts/estimates.

B
- Timeliness of notification of new hires to IT organization (i.e., within order lead-time window).
- Accuracy of information provided regarding new hire (e.g., planned start date, location, group, role/position, class of user).

C
- Timeliness of PC order for specific new hire.
- Accuracy of information provided regarding specific new hire (e.g., actual start date, location, group, role/position, class of user, special requirements).

D
- Level of orders delivered within time window and with zero defects.
- Timeliness of order deliveries.
- Timeliness of resolution of rejected orders.

E
- Timeliness of notification of leasing company to secure PC lease.
- Accuracy of information provided to leasing company.
- Timeliness of payment of vendor invoices for PCs.

F
- Timeliness of preparation, imaging, and testing process.
- Level of PCs with zero defects after preparation, imaging, and testing.

G
- Timeliness of providing PC leases.
- Accuracy of leases provided.

H
- Timeliness of PC entry into asset management system.
- Accuracy of data entered into asset management system.

I
- Level of PCs deployed on the agreed-on deployment date.
- Level of zero defects on deployment/installation.
- Timeliness of resolving deployment/installation problems.

J
- Level of user certifications issued resulting from participation in approved PC training.
- Various help desk call/service metrics by individual.

K
- Help desk incidents by business unit, type/category, location, individual.
- Help desk pick-up/resolution time by business unit, type/category, time of day, week, month.
- Level of abandoned calls.

L
- Break/fix maintenance by business unit, type/category, PC manufacturer, individual.
- Break/fix maintenance response/resolution time by type/category, PC manufacturer, location, individual.
- Level of unplanned emergency swaps required.

M
- Timeliness of notification of planned swaps and upgrades.
- Number of swaps performed daily, weekly, monthly by business unit, location.
- User satisfaction ratings regarding the swap process.

N
- Timeliness of notification of leasing company of retirement of PC.
- Timeliness of retirement of PC from asset management records.
- Quality of PC decommissioning process (software and data removal).

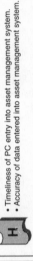

Figure 6.7 Sourcing/Partnering: Overall Flow Example—Total Spend Analysis (TSA)/Metrics.

static/steady-state service metrics continue to be appropriate and help ensure that ongoing service levels are maintained.

For example, static/steady-state service metrics are appropriate when a company is upgrading all of its PCs, but not the fundamental underlying software used by the business units. To ensure that these business applications are performing "as usual," static/steady-state service level metrics need to be maintained and monitored for the software.

However, the parts of the IT organization that are in the middle of executing the PC changeover and implementing new desktop software (and the people on the help desk) will experience a spike of unique activity and levels of effort. Therefore, static metrics will not suffice to measure this effort. Dynamic, project-management metrics that allow for the measurement of special transition activities and performance (e.g., detailed project milestone metrics, ramp-up and staging metrics) are needed.

Once past the transition period, all measurement can be transferred to steady-state metrics. Understanding this cycle is key to using performance metrics effectively in the constantly evolving and often rapidly changing IT environment. One of the most successful IT integration efforts I have seen was driven by a set of transition metrics developed by the CIO. These focused on effecting specific IT organizational, process, resource, and technology changes. The CIO was able to get the two merging IT organizations to focus only on those actions that helped to achieve the ultimate integration objective.

IT Organization Metrics

Most metrics in an IT organization focus on performance of the technology, hardware, software, and service infrastructure. Most CIOs consider these the *hard* metrics.

As fiscal and budgetary concerns rise to the fore, certain management and control measurements should be used to focus on the spend and cost issues. These can be embedded into the IT measurement mosaic. In addition, as greater attention is given to IT business value metrics, those, too, will begin to take a more prominent position on the CIO dashboard.

However, one area is often neglected in IT organization measurement: the set of measures related to the organization itself and to the people who comprise one of the largest components of the IT spend. CIOs typically give the least attention to these so-called "soft" metrics.

For a long time, CIOs have looked at head count, full-time equivalent (FTE), and retention/turnover measures. But those do not really provide much information about the real health of the IT organization and its members. The types of measures that are really needed here are those that focus on issues such as:

- The rate of movement and mix of IT skills, compared to the business objectives.
- The ability of the IT organization to continue to grow and evolve its skills base to accommodate new and changing technologies and business needs.
- The total compensation (base, individual and team bonuses, and market premiums) needed to change behaviors in the IT organization.
- The leverage effect of teaming as an IT organizational imperative.
- The overall IT organization morale and the ability of the IT organization to continue effectively to absorb and cope with continuous change.

When the CIO recognizes that the *people factor* is one of the most important drivers of the IT organization, he or she will ensure that IT organizational metrics are one of the first things looked at when perusing the CIO dashboard.

IT professionals at one company with which I worked believed that they were addressing the IT people factor because they traced monthly IT staff turnover statistics. What they failed to realize was that they were actually measuring the symptom of the problem rather than the root causes of their basic IT people and turnover issues. When they added several additional people measures that directly focused on progress in skills enhancement, movement and opportunity in compensation, teaming objectives, and satisfaction with IT supervisors, they were able to obtain a much clearer picture of the total set of IT people issues with which they needed to deal.

Relationship Metrics

Business-unit liaisons (BULs) are measured on the effectiveness of relationships they develop and maintain with the business-unit leadership and users. They are responsible for being the good cop to the CIO's bad cop in the relationship between the IT organization and each business unit or corporate department.

In addition to anecdotal critiques of the BUL's behavior toward business-unit personnel, a few objective metrics exist among the metric sets (dynamic and static) that reflect the type of relationship the BUL has developed.

Because BULs are, in essence, account managers, typical account management metrics can be used to measure their performance. Specific relationship management information can often be obtained through surveys that provide tactical data points, including the number of issues and frequency of issues handled by the BUL, the speed with which he or she is able to resolve issues, and user satisfaction around specific items. However, the true measure of a relationship, certainly from a long-term view, needs to be evaluated from a broader perspective.

The primary measure of the relationship between a BUL and a business unit is the extent to which the BUL enables the business unit to meet its strategic objectives by smoothing out any friction between the business unit and the IT organization. This can be looked at from service, problem-solving, crisis resolution, budgetary/financial, overall performance, and needs identification perspectives.

In addition, the effectiveness of the relationship is often measured based on the business unit's perception of the BUL and his or her abilities in myriad ways, including:

- Technical/functional expertise
- Perspective, understanding, and sensitivity toward business-unit (or corporate-departmental) issues
- Results-oriented leadership and facilitation capabilities
- Creativity and flexibility in leveraging solutions
- Speed of resolving issues
- Dedication and commitment to top-quality service and to meeting customer expectations
- Communications and relationship building.

From an IT perspective, the ultimate negative results of relationship problems are usually manifested in high levels of business unit and user dissatisfaction. One IT organization I assisted had spent little time developing, nurturing, and sustaining key customer/user relationships. They were perennially both surprised and disappointed over the results of a technology user survey conducted annually at the company. Once the CIO and IT organization were forced to take a deeper look at the issues, they realized that if they focused on the key relationship drivers associated with user satisfaction metrics (e.g., communicating, sensitivity toward the business unit's issues, speed of resolving issues), they would be able to impact the results more positively over time.

WHAT THE CEO CAN DO TO ENSURE THAT IT PERFORMANCE MEASUREMENT IS INTEGRAL TO IT MANAGEMENT

Ensuring desired IT outcomes is a complex process. Some of the complexity can be addressed through the consistent and disciplined application and use of performance metrics. However, the application and use of metrics must be focused and relevant for the performance measurement process to be effective.

CEOs can take five concrete steps to ensure that IT performance measurement becomes an integral part of overall IT management:

1. Make sure that the CIO is focusing not only on operational IT metrics, but also on relevant IT management and control and IT business value metrics.
2. Stress the importance of IT business value metrics to ensure that a meaningful dialogue is established between the CIO and other company executives. Ensure that the dialogue is a constructive one so the metrics are not used simply as a "whip."
3. Make sure that an integrated approach is being taken concerning IT performance measurement and that all areas of the IT management lens are included in some manner on the CIO's dashboard.
4. Direct the CIO to make sure that IT metrics at all levels are properly owned, transparent, and fully communicated across the company to provide a basis for achieving improvement.
5. Team the CIO with a business–unit CEO or other functional leader who is particularly adept in the use of performance measurement so that the CIO can learn how to use metrics more effectively in the IT organization.

CHAPTER 7

Leveraging Investment Cycles and the Power of Standardization

Choosing a Cost Model That Reduces Spend and Improves Productivity

After she spent her first year stabilizing a previously unstable IT environment, a CIO who was brought in to transform IT paused to reflect on the future. Although things were moving in the right direction, it was obvious to her that the company's cobbled together and fragmented IT infrastructure had to be completely overhauled and replaced to accommodate the volume, speed, and new requirements rapidly converging on it.

The company, whose primary business was information services, had a workforce that was increasingly mobile and that increasingly needed "anytime, anywhere" access to the company's IT systems. The CIO established an ambitious strategy and a set of plans to gut the old, inflexible, inefficient, and inherently high-cost infrastructure and to replace it with one that was more flexible.

The CIO recognized that incremental approaches to technology investments in the current IT infrastructure were never going to solve the fundamental problems that had developed over many years. Like many other companies, this one had made significant technology investments in good economic times and reduced those investments in bad times, regardless of the company's ever-present need to improve technology to enhance performance.

She assembled a team to work on defining and creating a workable architecture for a new companywide IT infrastructure. This new infrastructure architecture focused on:

- Creating *key centers* of IT hardware and service-based resources that would reduce redundant hardware and resources in each of the company's more than 75 locations. They would also drive economies of scale and cost effectiveness and include backup/ redundancy capabilities.
- Redesigning wide-area networks (WANs) and local-area networks (LANs) to create anytime, anywhere access to the company's networks.
- Reducing by two-thirds the number of servers necessary to support the key centers.
- Directing Internet access in a secure manner through officially commissioned firewalls.
- Developing a virtual private network (VPN) for dial-in situations to reduce dial-in costs radically and improve security and efficiency.

Implementing this set of infrastructure solutions was extremely expensive, but the CIO and her program design team justified the implementation by showing the cost savings and productivity enhancements that the total reconstitution of the infrastructure would provide.

Implementation of an expensive and expansive infrastructure redevelopment program, such as the one described previously, is a point-in-time capital expenditure akin to building a new manufacturing plant. Funding for such a program must be justified by showing a real payback over time.

Unfortunately, too many companies treat all IT investments in this way, forcing CIOs and IT staffs to develop a justification for every purchase. In reality, much of the hardware and software in any company's IT environment has a life cycle of less than three years before it becomes technologically obsolete, placing those using the system at a competitive disadvantage.

IT leaders operating in a *capital expense* IT environment are constantly working up economic justifications for each expenditure, which cuts into the time they have for understanding how the IT strategy meshes with the business strategy and for effectively managing the IT organization.

To move to a normal cost model of IT expenditures, corporate leaders need to look beyond accounting rules and disentangle IT costs from the business cycle. This entails envisioning IT costs as annual, rather than capital, costs. Even in cases where the IT costs cannot be removed from the balance sheet (in an accounting sense), they need to be removed from the capital expense ledger (in a business planning sense).

A COST OF DOING BUSINESS

The cost of maintaining current information technology is simply a cost of doing business, a cost that existed only to a lesser extent before the mid-1980s and the advent of the personal computer. As more and more employees use more and more IT, that cost continues to rise.

Removing IT spending from the vagaries of the business cycle normalizes the rate at which cost increases occur, that is, the up and down spikes of annual expenditures that occur when IT is considered a capital expense, and the cost of work that goes into the implementation of any IT asset. The objective is to make IT spend as stable and efficient as possible.

In the following example of a *desktop renewal,* we see how costs occur in a capital expense model and in an ongoing expense model. In this scenario, the company has 10,000 employees, all of whom work in stationary offices and use desktop computers. The computers are all becoming obsolete and must be replaced.

The Cap-Ex Model

In the capital expense (cap-ex) model, a purchase of 10,000 new desktop computers would have to be justified at, for example, $2,000 per unit, or $20 million. To justify a $20 million expenditure, a CIO would have to show how the purchase of these computers would improve personal productivity or processes such that an adequate payback or ROI would be available in the same year as the purchase.

However, what never surfaces in this capital request is the cost of staff hours as they unpack and test the hardware, install any necessary software, burn in any companywide images, install the hardware on desks, assist employees to get accustomed to the new hardware and upgraded software, transfer any applications software or data from the old machines to the new machines, and a host of other activities. Such additional soft costs typically add somewhere between 30 and 50 percent of the purchase price of the new equipment on top of the base capital expenditure.

Over the next two-to-three years, as these desktop computers become older and, gradually, obsolete, the cost of service increases each year. In addition, as the technology falls further behind the cutting edge, employee efficiency and productivity fall further behind best-in-class benchmarks. Ultimately, the CIO must ask executive leadership for yet another desktop renewal, a request that will compete with other capital expense requests.

A number of companies I have worked with in different industries have turned the IT capital expenditure request-and-approval process into something akin to an art form, expending all of this effort just to purchase a PC that probably costs less than the desk at which the person is sitting. In this case, the overhead cost associated with maintaining the capital expenditure policing process is, without question, greater than the value of the PC.

Such a stop/start model consumes a great deal of time among those who must justify the equipment purchases and does not reflect the reality

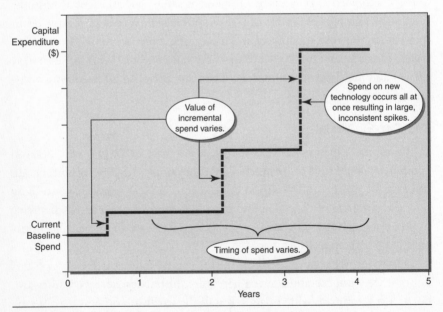

Figure 7.1   Capital Expenditure Model.

of how PCs are used in today's business environment. The spend impact of such a model is illustrated in Figure 7.1.

The cap-ex model also has a detrimental impact on the IT organization's staffing, in that it creates staff load pyramids whenever a new purchase of PCs is made (see Figure 7.2). Staffing must grow to accommodate increases in activity related to increases in the acquisition of new technology over and above the other functions of an IT staff that must be maintained. Once the work activity level related to the new technology purchase declines, the staffing level declines as well.

The IT organization must take one of three steps to accommodate such spikes in staffing needs:

1. Reduce the amount of work that staff members perform on other IT efforts, possibly causing a reduction in service levels.
2. Ask IT staff to work enormous amounts of extra time to accommodate the spike in demand for implementation of the new technology while maintaining constant service levels on ongoing IT efforts.
3. Contract in extra resources.

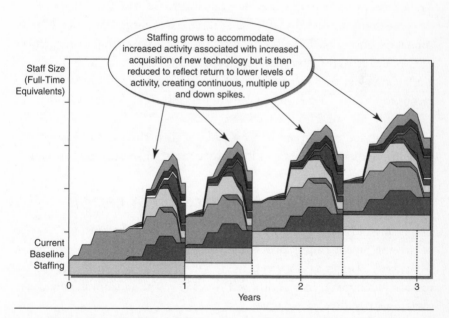

Figure 7.2   Staff Load Pyramid: Capital Expenditure Model.

None of these options is optimal. The first can harm relationships between the IT organization and users, as well as between the company and its customers and business partners; the second can lead to staff burnout; and the third can be very expensive and difficult to manage and result in inconsistent quality.

The Annual Expense Model

Using the annual expense model, the number of desktop computers—in this case, 10,000—is divided by the average life cycle of a desktop. Depending on the types of work performed on these computers, this life cycle usually runs two or three years. This means that somewhere between 3,000 and 5,000 computers need to be replaced each year, reducing the purchase cost from $20 million in one year to a cost of either approximately $6.7 million a year or $10 million a year.

In addition, the extra workload for IT staff who must perform the desktop upgrades is reduced by a similar amount, that is, either by one-half or by two-thirds. This means less overtime, fewer temporary outside resources to assist with this effort, or more time for staff to devote to other important IT work. Figure 7.3 illustrates how, over time, the annual expense model effectively smoothes out the expenditure for new technology.

One company I know well did such an excellent job of moving to an annual expense model for PCs that within a year of starting, management had decided to move most of the company's servers and a fair amount of network equipment onto the same model. Their purpose was to smooth out the spend, to establish more predictable annual cash flow requirements for IT, and to stay current with the technology curve.

Leasing and outsourcing are two additional alternatives that can, potentially, drive the provisioning of PCs further toward an ongoing cost basis.

LEASING HELPS MANAGE RAPID TECHNOLOGY CHANGE

Dispersing purchases of new desktop computers over the normal life cycle of the equipment helps management change its view of PC provisioning from considering it a capital expense to viewing it as an expense more akin to normal, ongoing, annual expenditures. However, no natural, predictable cycle for upgrading exists as yet.

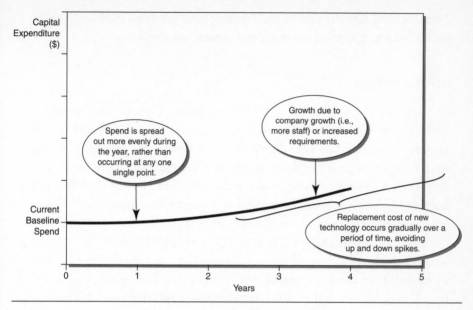

Figure 7.3   Annual Expense Model.

Leasing enables companies to review their PC technology base at regular intervals—when the lease expires—without incurring large cyclical spikes in capital expenditures. This, in turn, allows companies to keep pace with rapidly changing technology while minimizing capital risk. By normalizing the PC technology spend, leasing drives companies to establish consistent annual budgets for technology and creates a regular, more stable, and predictable cycle for replacing aging technology.

Finally, leasing requires that a company implement discipline and processes for asset management because all PCs must be accounted for and ultimately returned to the lessor. Although leasing PCs might be more costly than purchasing because of the difference in financing costs, one school of thought is that over time, leasing actually lowers the total spend for PC *ownership*.

Management of a large multinational media content company I have worked with decided that using a leasing approach would save the company more than the value of the finance costs incurred by reducing PC inventory costs and handling charges. The discipline of having to return all of the company's PCs at the end of the leasing cycle was the catalyst needed to streamline the PC acquisition and retirement processes.

OUTSOURCING

Outsourcing the provisioning of PCs transforms more of the cost of the desktop renewal into an ongoing cost but only when the company outsources the process and not just the product. Under purchasing or leasing, the product coming in the door and IT staff must perform the setup. Under outsourcing, the provider delivers a completely functional PC, where it is needed, when it is needed, in accordance with the specified guidelines provided by the company.

Because certain processes, such as PC provisioning, are fairly pervasive across multiple organizations, many companies look at these processes as non-value-added commodities whose costs can be lowered by outsourcing. Companies looking to reduce PC provisioning costs, improve operational effectiveness, free up IT staff for more value-added efforts, and improve user satisfaction levels often outsource the provisioning of PCs. Some outsourcers have taken this concept to the next level, offering a one-stop, per-head, full-scope (e.g., PC provisioning, service, maintenance, replacement, asset management) PC utility service arrangement.

Because outsourcing is a negotiated arrangement, clients can build in whatever level of flexibility the company desires, in essence buying services *by the pound*.

In difficult economic times, obtaining PCs and PC services using a by-the-pound outsourcing arrangement can provide a company with maximum flexibility for workforce reductions. Because outsourcing entails no residual lease costs or costs associated with the disposal of purchased PCs, clients can create an arrangement whereby the company can turn on and turn off the flow of PCs based on need.

DRIVING TOWARD STANDARDIZATION

As companies move away from the capital expense model of at least some IT hardware and software purchasing, they remove the constant state of variability concerning new technology acquisitions and force some key technology management practices to be adopted. Certain of these practices—

including establishing *classes of use* and asset management processes, and forecasting technology growth needs and staffing increases (or decreases)—contribute to creating an environment that facilitates mass or class standardization.

However, standardization is a relative state. Because of the rapidly changing pace of technology, standardization applies most to the acquisition process, the current technology footprint, and the overall upward migration path. Nevertheless, moving away from a capital expense model to an annual expense model provides the foundation necessary to achieve greater leverage and benefits from standardization.

LEVERAGING THE POWER OF STANDARDIZATION

The virtues of standardization are intuitive. And when they are synthesized, they lead to two consequences: reduced costs per unit of activity and reduced aggregate costs associated with the standardized item (e.g., break/fix maintenance of a PC) over a specified time period. This means that the same amount of work can be done for less (if the company is in a cost-cutting mode), or more work can be done for the same cost (if the company is in a growth mode). It also means that the reductions achieved can be both sustainable and consistent over a given period of time. The advantages of standardized processes and technology include:

- *Standardized processes:* If everyone follows the same processes, good things happen. For instance, people can fill in for one another if the need arises; they can move from job to job within the same department, across business units, or across departments in the company; they can teach newly hired employees or those new to the department. Although the specifics of a task might be different, the way it's carried out is the same.
- *Standardized technology:* If everyone uses the same equipment (e.g., standardized PCs), the help desk, break/fix maintenance, software, and training can be standardized. Again, this means being able to do more with less total human resources.

But truly standardizing technology across a large, complex, and even global company means going far beyond simply providing each employee with a standard desktop or laptop computer. A fully standardized IT organization will normalize the platform (servers, storage, etc.), the "plumbing" (the network and telecommunications infrastructure), the processes used to carry out enhancements to the IT environment, the metrics used to measure both static service levels and dynamic efforts, and the relationship between the IT organization and its constituents in the corporate departments and operating business units.

This total standardization of processes and technology allows the IT organization to achieve both flexibility and agility. At any of the companies I have worked with, IT executives, after standardizing some aspect of the company's IT capability (typically PCs, servers, or applications), often complained about not getting the synergies they expected. More often than not, they stopped with the hardware and software and neglected to standardize the processes, measurements, and relationships.

CASE STUDY 7.2

Squeezing Out IT Synergies

A highly decentralized company in the communications industry had embarked on a massive *growth by acquisition* strategy, making more than 100 acquisitions in just a few years. Because of the company's independent and decentralized structure, managers at these acquired entities, as well as at the company's original business units, were encouraged to act independently and to use their own initiative to create revenue.

Such a fiercely competitive culture worked against identifying any synergies or economies of scale in IT or in other departmental functions that could have been consolidated across the enterprise.

When the global economy began to soften, revenues at all of the company's independent operating entities began to suffer, and corporate leadership realized the need to begin looking for consolidation of non-customer-facing functions to achieve economies of scale.

About the same time corporate leadership was coming to this realization, the company engaged in one final, very large acquisition of a company that had already consolidated many of its accounting systems into a shared services environment. Using this new acquisition's prior work as a model, the company embarked on an effort to consolidate into several large divisions and to collapse all of the formerly independent entities' IT into a more centralized IT organization.

An outside advisor was brought in to assist with the process. Because of the significant number of individual, decentralized companies and the general lack of focus on IT costs throughout the company, a decision was made to focus on the largest operating units that comprised the bulk of the IT spend (i.e., to follow the 80/20 rule).

A common approach was developed to capture detailed data about the IT spend by major category across these large operating units. At the same time, the advisor reviewed the management, organization, operations, budgeting processes, and IT infrastructure in each of the major businesses. Profiles were created for each that described the IT spend, key IT management processes, IT assets, and IT resources.

A review of these profiles surfaced multiple redundancies and duplications of functions, assets, people, and processes; an inherently high and ever-increasing cost structure; an imbalance in service levels available to users of the different operating units; and an infrastructure that could not support management's growth goals for the company. It was impossible to identify and assign costs to all of the IT assets because only limited IT asset records and a minimum of IT financial information existed.

The advisor developed an approach to move the organization from a highly fragmented environment to one that would be fully shared and then outsourced. The approach involved four stages:

1. Identify the key issues and get control of the situation.
2. Rationalize, contain, and standardize the IT environment.
3. Establish shared services at the corporate and divisional levels.
4. Move forward with selective outsourcing or partnering.

In the second phase—rationalization and standardization—standards were to be driven within the context of replaceable IT processes that, where lacking, were identified or defined. The focus would be on broad improvement efforts rather than individual projects, on identification of key dependencies, on the establishment of detailed targets and goals, and on development of key performance metrics. In this way, underlying processes—rather than hardware and software alone—would be acknowledged as the key factors that would truly allow the company to take advantage of the leveraging of information that can be attained through use of IT.

In addition, the company could not move to a shared services environment until processes and systems were standardized. Also, if the company, rather than the outsourcing provider, were to reap the benefits of change, internal processes and systems needed to be standardized.

THREE STEPS TO FULL STANDARDIZATION

To move to a fully standardized IT environment, a company needs to understand the relevance of standardization to three key components:

1. Technology support
2. Information enhancement
3. Strategic enabling.

This relevance is illustrated in Figure 7.4.

As a company's IT operations move across this *standards continuum* from left to right, they advance from areas of IT where standardization is easiest to achieve across multiple business units in a company to areas where there are limitations to achieving any substantive standardization.

Typically, the *technology support* component demonstrates the most commonality (among, for example, technology infrastructure-related items) and typically elicits the least resistance to standardization. Once everyone agrees that it is permissible to standardize around technology support items, the process of moving in that direction can be accelerated, facilitated, and driven.

In the *information enhancement* component, across-the-board standardization is harder to pursue, particularly for certain types of applications. For example, although standard financial and HR software packages are relatively easy to pursue, it is far more difficult to standardize the individual customer-facing systems that exist in each business unit, even if one package would suit the needs of all the business units. Although standardizing the information enhancement component is important, IT managers must be sensitive to push-back from business units that consider themselves and their applications unique. The benefits of standardization are simply not worth the organizational battles that often ensue.

Finally, standardization is hardest to pursue with the *strategic enabling* component. Often, it cannot be achieved at all because of the unique qualities of this component's technology. The strategic enabling component

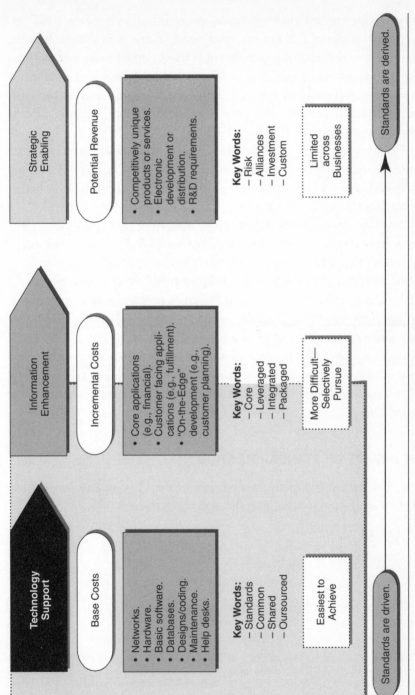

Figure 7.4 IT Standards Continuum.

very often involves high investments in new technologies or new technology-based business models that can ultimately result in revenue creation. In many cases, the strategic enabling component is unique to an individual business unit and cannot be standardized and leveraged elsewhere in the company. Although standardization can be accomplished to some degree, the standards are usually not clear from the start and, therefore, must be evolved (derived) over a period of time.

For companies with multiple business units, technology spend can occur at any point on the IT standards continuum. The challenge is to understand where each aspect of the technology portfolio sits and to determine whether standardization would be relevant.

To fully appreciate the benefits derivable from standardization, companies must develop a good knowledge of their total IT spend and of the unit costs of each of the various IT assets in their portfolios.

In addition, companies must also be aware of the costs that occur *as a result* of standardization. One of the virtues of standardization is that it eliminates the need for much of a company's legacy IT hardware and software, since companies tend to upgrade as they do it. As a result, many IT personnel whose skill sets revolved around legacy systems will either have to be retrained or be removed (both options are costly). In addition, new IT personnel with new skill sets will need to be hired and compensated at market rates.

THE IMPACT OF STANDARDIZATION

Typically, within any of the components of the IT standards continuum, the standardization process goes through three stages:*

1. Foundation
2. Consolidation
3. Leverage.

At each stage, a different impact can be identified.

---

* In discussing the process of moving a company through the three phases of standardization, I will focus on the work of the CIO of a global information services company and on the impact of standardization using an example related to the Technology Support component of the IT Standards Continuum.

Foundation

Foundation technology is that which establishes the basic and common infrastructure on which a company can cost-effectively run its systems, process its data, and communicate internally and externally. Foundation technology is not the glamorous or slick dot-com, Web-based technology. Rather, it is the plumbing of the company's technology. People do not really notice it much when it is working, and they expect it to be working perfectly all of the time. However, when it doesn't work, even for just a short while, the effects can be disastrous.

Foundation is the bread-and-butter standardization that most companies pursue. For all but those companies for which information technology is core to their business model or a key aspect of their product (e.g., media, pure e-business, financial services, or information services), the foundation step, when executed well, will deliver many of a company's total standardization benefits, including as much as 60 percent of its potential cost savings and 30 percent of its potential service improvements.

In addition, the more a company standardizes its IT environment, the more it will be able to take advantage of that standardization to leverage future gains. Although this might seem self-evident, I cannot count the number of times I have seen companies standardize certain aspects of their IT environment and then not follow through and leverage that standardization by driving ahead with other programs. For example, they standardize by buying the same model PC, create a standard desktop image and platform, and stop there because they think they have standardized. The real benefits of standardization kick in when the company uses the standardized PC image to gain other benefits such as pushing out new software easily and quickly to everyone, restructuring the help desk to make it easier to use with the new PCs, or allowing help desk people to capture users' PCs online and conduct diagnostics and solve problems. These downstream items or leverage are where the real gains are achieved, well beyond the initial act of standardization. Three large pieces of technology foundation can be standardized. Each block increases the value derived from the standardization and moves forward the starting points from which further value will be added by the second and third stages.

The first level of value is obtained from standardizing PCs. This includes standardizing the seven elements illustrated in Figure 7.5.

194

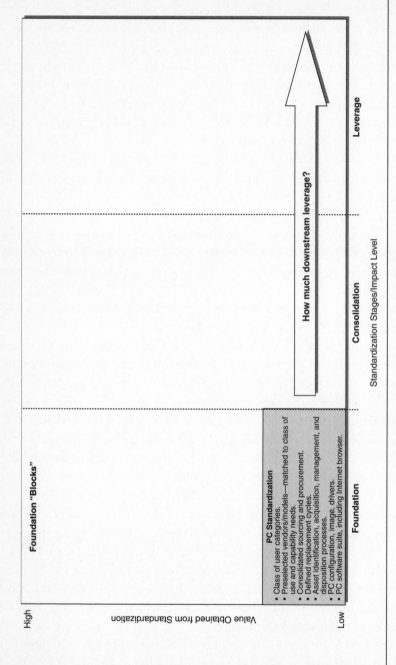

Figure 7.5 Impact of IT Standardization: PC.

The second block of standardization involves infrastructure. This block includes eight more elements, as illustrated in Figure 7.6. Finally, services, the third block of standardization, adds yet another eight elements, which are illustrated in Figure 7.7.

Objections to standardization sometimes arise among those who think that *standardized* is another word for a one size fits all. The best standardization efforts analyze user needs and develop a small number (e.g., five to seven) of broad yet manageable categories of need into which all users can be placed. These classes of use can then be layered on each other so that everyone uses the same basic PC shell, operating system, and foundation software package. For those who are in a higher class of use, that is, those who need more sophisticated software, more memory, or more storage capacity, the extras can be layered on top of the basics.

Many companies with which I have worked have failed to draw the distinction between *one size fits all* and *class of use.* When this failure occurs, standardization efforts often become bloody battlefields, with much of the fighting taking place around issues that are not relevant. The best solutions I have seen are the ones that get a company on the right path toward managing the process of standardization by ensuring adequate flexibility to accommodate normal differences among the different classes of users.

Costs can be attached not only to the procurement of different boxes for different classes of users, but also to the degree of support required for each one of those boxes. For example, if one business unit has assigned 200 employees to the highest class of use and another business unit has assigned only 50 employees to that class, one would think that the first business unit would be responsible for four times as many help desk requests as the other business unit, directly as a result of just having more PCs in that class. However, that may, in fact, not always be the case. Other factors, such as what software the users in each business unit regularly employ, the typical complexities in the nature of their help desk requests, how mobile users are, and what type of user training they receive must also be understood. These additional factors, which may be different for each business unit, will have a direct and tangible impact on the true class of use and the resultant downstream total costs.

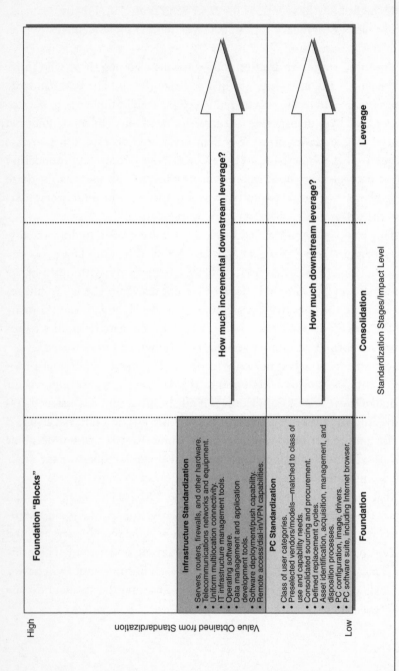

Figure 7.6   Impact of IT Standardization: Infrastructure.

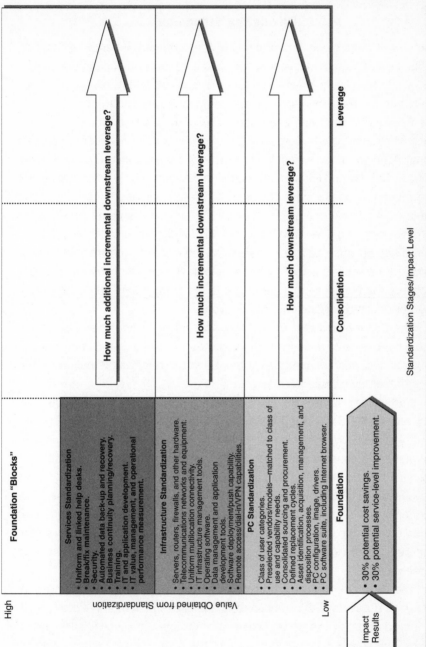

Figure 7.7   Impact of IT Standardization: Services.

CASE STUDY 7.3

Driving the Standards

The new CIO of a global information services company inherited a situation concerning PC standards; acquisition, configuration, and deployment of PCs; the ability to provide break/fix maintenance; and help desk support that could best be described as erratic, chaotic, and very costly.

Because of the fragmented way in which IT had been run in the past, each of the company's more than 55 offices made independent decisions about PC type, models, software, networks, maintenance, and help desk service. Nobody had initiated any action to take advantage of the company's enormous purchasing power by aggregating the purchase of products and services. A number of employees worked on their own laptops at one of the company's other offices. The local help desk was often unable to help these individuals because help desk personnel did not deal with the hardware or software they were using. If the local help desk staff were able to solve the problem, the employee might go back to his or her home office only to encounter difficulty logging onto the network.

The CIO realized that driving IT standardization into the organization would be a key step in accomplishing downstream economies, efficiencies, cost savings, and service improvements and in removing IT pain from the lives of technology users.

Nothing to improve the situation could be accomplished until the second year of the CIO's plan, at which point he hoped to have gained some control of the IT organization and to have received from corporate leadership a mandate to consolidate IT into a single organization under his authority. Even so, he still had to convince local office management and local IT employees that doing things together in a consistent way would make progress easier and less costly. He also had to convince the local IT staffs that jobs would not be lost by turning over much of the effort of PC procurement and support to outside contractors who possessed core competence in those areas.

The CIO commissioned a comprehensive analysis, including an inventory of all IT assets in the company and an assessment of the related needs of individual business units, broad user groups, and individual high-end users. This analysis revealed that all of the company's PC users could be grouped into five logical classes of use. Each class of use identified key characteristics of the user group that determined the appropriate size, power, and speed of the PC, as well as the peripherals that would match their needs over the next two years. In addition, the analysis described the unique software—outside the standard word processing, spreadsheet, and presentation suite—specific to each class of use.

Development of these classes of use radically streamlined the manner in which the company dealt with both business units and outside vendors. It simplified the ordering, configuration, and deployment of hardware and software. A companywide standard image was developed in consultation with business-unit leaders, and the decision was made that individuals would keep a machine for two years before receiving a new machine with any necessary upgrades. A lease-versus-buy analysis conducted by an outside finance company determined that leasing was the most appropriate financial alternative.

The two-year leasing cycle provided corollary benefits in the areas of asset management and control. It also provided a trigger point for asset retirement and, therefore, a natural control point for asset management.

A 24/7 companywide help desk was established to replace the various help arrangements that local offices had previously employed (or not employed, as the case may have been). These included in-house help, outsourced help, or no help at all. A single help desk solution allowed for the collection and analysis of uniform data, statistics, and performance measures that could drive improvement in many areas. No help desk metrics had yet been developed with which to measure the performance of the third-party help desk service. But other measures captured the volume of help desk calls by different departments and business units in the company or by different classes of use. Such information helped drive improvements in user training and facilitated the identification of trends and potential problem areas.

Because of its high-touch nature, break/fix maintenance remained a local office challenge; but because of PC standardization, local offices were able more easily to replace PCs as appropriate to different classes of use.

Once individuals, offices, corporate departments, and business units had helped to define the parameters of the various classes of use, the CIO became the point of contact with the outside vendors who performed the procurement, configuration and delivery of computers, and the help desk, leaving local IT staff free to focus on customer service, support, and execution.

The CIO established a partnering relationship with third-party vendors. Together, the CIO and the top business executives of the vendors involved developed executive working principles. These principles were used to guide the actions and behavior of all parties. In addition, jointly developed performance metrics created transparency across all activities and enabled everyone involved to focus on improvements instead of on blame, sidestepping the finger-pointing that is the norm in many outsourcing relationships.

As a result of these efforts, the IT organization physically "touched," cataloged, standardized, converted, and upgraded more than 10,000 PCs over a four-month period. PC and related standards, performance metrics, and processes allowed the IT organization to lay the foundation for streamlining other parts of the IT environment. Creating a partnering relationship with outside vendors enabled the IT organization to free up resources to engage in more complex IT initiatives that could leverage the standardization efforts.

Finally, members of the IT organization began to realize that working together as a team was powerful and that the IT organization could operate at a high level of professionalism and accomplish complex efforts in a high-performance manner.

Consolidation

As Figures 7.5, 7.6, and 7.7 indicate, when each of the foundation blocks is put into place, a certain amount of benefit concerning efficiencies and economies can be achieved. However, even greater benefits and synergies are achieved when the activities and efforts contained in each block are effectively integrated. This stage of standardization can be described as *consolidation*.

As the individual component aspects and benefits of each foundation block are brought together, the groundwork is laid for achieving even greater efficiencies and economies. For example, PC standardization alone is not sufficient. True, standardizing PCs can reduce the costs of acquisition, deployment, and maintenance. But only by standardizing services, infrastructure, *and* PCs can the power of standardization be truly leveraged.

When IT professionals address the infrastructure and service blocks at the same time as they address the basic technology, the resulting consolidation leverages all of the individual benefits. Under this service block arrangement, employees throughout the organization receive not only new PCs, but also a guarantee that, in the event a PC breaks down, a functional replacement will be provided. The block arrangement extends to infrastructure. Employees can also receive continuous backups of their hard drives automatically each time they connect.

Figure 7.8 illustrates the impact and benefits related to foundation stage standardization that begin to accrue in the consolidation stage. The higher the number of blocks laid in the foundation stage, the steeper the benefits slope in the consolidation stage.

CASE STUDY 7.4
Building on and Consolidating the Foundation

As a result of the new CIO's first efforts at standardization, the company had standardized its PCs into five classes of users, ranging from those who worked in one location on a small suite of software applications to those who were highly mobile, used far more sophisticated software applications, and needed to send and receive large volumes of data and information over the company's network.

Although the standardization of PCs and application software allowed these individuals to receive technical assistance at any of the company's locations or customer sites, the company's infrastructure still was not capable of handling the large and ever-growing volume of use. And the infrastructure still needed to be scaled up to accommodate additional capabilities. The current infrastructure was based on an assumption that professionals and staff worked in a static office environment. However, the business strategy envisioned that the company's workforce very rapidly would become highly mobile.

Individuals who needed to connect to their base office servers from other office locations, would have to locate fax machines, disconnect and reconnect them to modems, connect their PCs to the modems, and then dial into one of the few modems in their home offices that were capable of receiving incoming calls and of streaming data.

The CIO realized that incremental approaches or technology investments made to the current IT infrastructure were never going to solve the

202

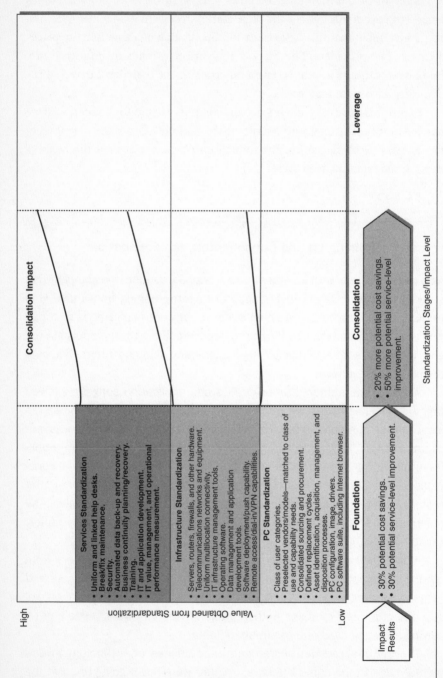

Figure 7.8　Impact of IT standardization: Foundation/Consolidation.

fundamental problems. He assembled a team of top IT strategy, architecture, and customer service professionals. To this team he added key users from each business unit. The group was charged with describing how the most highly mobile members of the professional staff would work in the future and the type of connectivity, access, storage, networking, backup/redundancy, speed, security, and technical help that they would need in such a work environment.

The new topography focused on clusters of key centers at which major networks of servers, routers, and other technology would be located, along with the critical mass of staff that possessed the right skills to serve them. These key centers reduced cost and improved service while eliminating approximately two-thirds of the servers that had been in use throughout the company and, by networking the servers, adding backup/redundancy capabilities.

In addition, the company's WANs and LANs were totally redesigned so that employees working at any company office in the world or at any of the major customer offices where employees were permanently located could plug into the network connection in the office and operate as if they were at their own desks. This redesign enabled users to weather catastrophic hard drive failures while out of the office. As long as they were at locations that were near other company offices, they could, in crisis situations, obtain functional replacements within one or two hours. In addition, automatic backups would make it possible to populate replacements with users' own data.

Leverage

After the consolidation stage is completed and all of the components are working together as they should, high-impact benefits begin to kick in. This occurs in the *leverage* stage. As all of the blocks come together, key processes related to each become more and more integrated, efficient, and cost effective.

For example, if company management decides to make a substantial acquisition or to drive rapid organic growth, the combination of the three technology support foundation blocks, fully consolidated, will enable the company fully and quickly to absorb the PC, infrastructure, and service demands of the new users, thus providing significant, geometric leverage and strategic and tactical benefits associated with the acquisition or with organic growth. Fundamentally, this demonstrates that investments made in technology support during the foundation stage and the consolidation stage (when some benefits are already occurring) are fully maximized during the leverage stage.

Figure 7.9 illustrates the incremental impact and benefits related to technology support standardization as they appear during the leverage stage, when the slopes continue to diverge.

CASE STUDY 7.5

Absorbing Change and Leveraging Results

The new CIO had already standardized PCs, the infrastructure, and services and had done an effective job of integrating these on a global basis for more than 30,000 employees. The next challenge related to a large acquisition driven by the company's CEO. This acquisition would almost double the size of the organization to about 55,000 employees.

What calmed the CIO was the knowledge that he and his company had already gone through the foundation and consolidation stages of technology support standardization. He believed he had the ability to absorb the impact of the acquisition effectively. What caused the CIO some concern was the fact that he had only several months in which to accomplish the IT integration for Day One of the postmerger environment.

In light of the small amount of time in which to plan and execute the IT integration, the standardization efforts that had already taken place proved to be invaluable. They enabled the CIO to leverage off everything he had previously accomplished. The CIO's initial focus was to work with the business units to establish Day One assumptions and priorities. These included:

- Exchanging PC documents across the entire organization
- Consolidating end-user support locally and regionally
- Developing a single e-mail environment
- Developing a single network
- Using the base already established, standardizing the PC configuration for as many people as quickly as possible

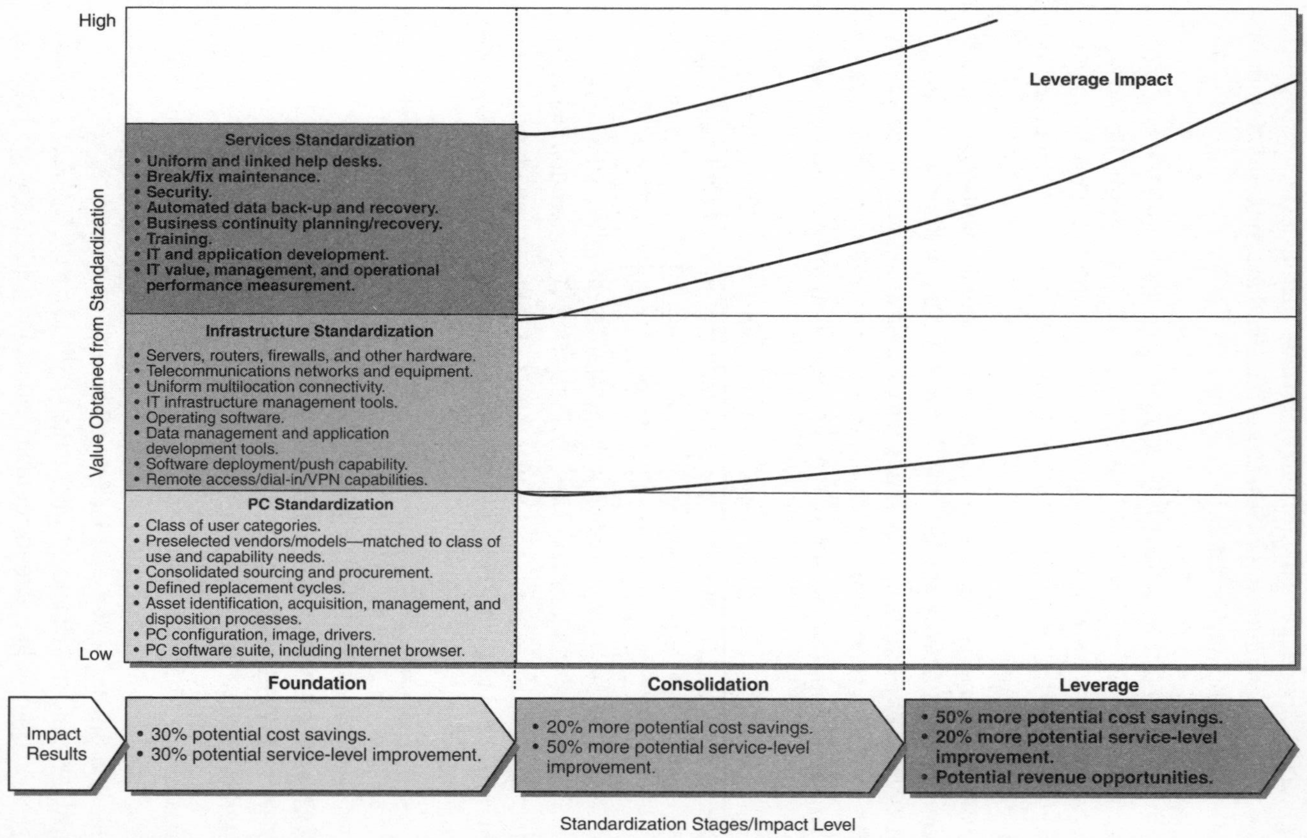

Services Standardization
- Uniform and linked help desks.
- Break/fix maintenance.
- Security.
- Automated data back-up and recovery.
- Business continuity planning/recovery.
- Training.
- IT and application development.
- IT value, management, and operational performance measurement.

Infrastructure Standardization
- Servers, routers, firewalls, and other hardware.
- Telecommunications networks and equipment.
- Uniform multilocation connectivity.
- IT infrastructure management tools.
- Operating software.
- Data management and application development tools.
- Software deployment/push capability.
- Remote access/dial-in/VPN capabilities.

PC Standardization
- Class of user categories.
- Preselected vendors/models—matched to class of use and capability needs.
- Consolidated sourcing and procurement.
- Defined replacement cycles.
- Asset identification, acquisition, management, and disposition processes.
- PC configuration, image, drivers.
- PC software suite, including Internet browser.

High

Low

Value Obtained from Standardization

Leverage Impact

Foundation
- 30% potential cost savings.
- 30% potential service-level improvement.

Consolidation
- 20% more potential cost savings.
- 50% more potential service-level improvement.

Leverage
- 50% more potential cost savings.
- 20% more potential service-level improvement.
- Potential revenue opportunities.

Impact Results

Standardization Stages/Impact Level

Figure 7.9   Impact of IT standardization: Leverage.

205

- Providing common voice- and video-conference services at key locations
- Providing common access to key applications systems and data across the new company.

Because so much work had already been completed on the standardization, the CIO had an excellent base in place to absorb, from a technology perspective, the newly acquired employees. Some tweaking would be necessary, but, for the most part, the CIO's integration plan was focused on leveraging the base.

One of his main concerns was having an adequate number of skilled IT resources to be able to address the volume of IT needs during the transition. Because he was able to leverage his existing standardized technology base, the CIO was able to reduce his resource requirements dramatically and to retool and retrain many of the IT people from the acquired company very quickly.

In addition, many of the technology standardization decisions that a CIO normally would have to make during an integration effort had already been made during the previous standardization work. Leveraging these previous decisions enabled the CIO to reduce significantly the time required for the integration. This reduction was imperative, given the small amount of time remaining before Day One. The Day One IT integration activities were a complete success, and a major part of that success could be directly attributed to the CIO's understanding and ability to drive and leverage standardization.

WHAT THE CEO CAN DO TO DISENGAGE IT COSTS FROM THE BUSINESS CYCLE AND TO LEVERAGE STANDARDIZATION

Transforming IT spend from a start/stop cycle of up and down spikes into a model that treats IT expenditures as normal and regular annual costs is a key element of managing IT as a business. There are a number of techniques available to smooth out and normalize the IT spend curve. Companies should implement approaches that ensure that critical IT spend items are fully insulated from the vicissitudes of the business cycle.

In addition, leveraging the power of standardization in most companies is no small undertaking. If done right, it is a detailed, time-consuming, and, for some, daunting task. But doing so is imperative if a company really wants to start the process of achieving fundamental IT spend management. CEOs can take five concrete steps to disengage IT costs from the business cycle and to leverage IT standardization across the organization:

1. Make sure the CIO has the proper support from the finance group to ensure that all economic and operational models for IT acquisitions and expenditures are considered, analyzed, and compared.

2. Focus the CIO and the business-unit leaders on understanding the effects of their technology acquisition decisions not only from a point-in-time perspective, but also from the perspective of the total IT spend over a period of time.

3. Make sure the CIO understands the three stages of standardization—foundation, consolidation, and leverage—and that he or she knows how best to apply them in the company.

4. Educate business unit leaders so that they will better understand the high multiplier effect that IT standardization can have on lowering total IT spend across the company.

5. Challenge business unit leaders to seek out and identify ways to standardize all aspects of IT they use and reward them for doing so. Help them to understand the positive downstream impact of IT standardization across the company.

Talk about Information Technology and Use IT Appropriately so Others Know It Is Important

Communicating as a Strategic IT Competency

Because of a fragmented IT structure that had developed over the years and because each local IT group was attempting to outdo the others, communication within the IT organization of a large, multibusiness-unit, North American food services company was severely limited. Compounding the problem was the fact that meaningful communication among members of the IT organization and other constituencies in the company was nonexistent. Any communication that did occur was brief, often "IT-cryptic," and usually self-serving.

Some IT leaders were so controlling that they overpowered their staffs, members of which already feared communicating with one another and with users. In such an atmosphere, communication within the IT organization was usually hierarchical and downward, taking the form of directives from on high, offering little chance for discussions around key issues. And, when it did occur at all, communication from the IT organization to outside constituencies was filtered through IT leadership.

IT leaders communicated poorly with the company's executive business-unit management. Even when the IT organization had accomplished great things that it could brag about, IT leadership's lack of understanding concerning the power of marketing and communications virtually ensured that nobody in the company was taking the IT organization seriously.

Fortunately, company leadership appointed a new CIO who understood the power of communication, both within the organization and between the organization and its constituencies. In the IT organization, he undertook a series of steps to begin the process of opening up lines of communication from IT leadership to staff, from IT staff to leadership, and among IT staff, so they could more effectively meet their users' needs:

- He set up a series of open, honest, and candid dialogues across IT and with IT users and business-unit management teams—an IT organization version of town hall sessions.
- He established an open door policy whereby anyone in the IT organization could communicate directly with him—face to face, over the telephone, or via e-mail. Part of this policy was an open electronic forum (similar to a chat room) where individuals could—anonymously if they wished—pose questions to their colleagues or to the CIO.
- He initiated a "no surprises" policy focused on encouraging people to communicate problems early so that they could leverage one another's expertise to find solutions before the problems grew larger.

He intuitively understood the power of marketing, even though he knew that he did not have all of the skills required to create and deliver effective marketing messages. He brought a professional marketing and communications person into the organization and asked that individual to help him and others throughout the IT organization to become more effective communicators among themselves, with users, and with business unit and corporate managers.

Communication does not just happen. It requires confidence on the part of the organization's leader and should incorporate professional assistance to tailor the organization's message for particular audiences. Each of the relationships between the CIO or other IT organization members and various stakeholders has a specific set of ongoing communication needs. And special messages—marketing campaigns, for example—must be crafted by the IT organization to facilitate particular implementation and rollout efforts or IT transitions.

The CIO sits at the center of a series of three open-ended communications channels or *funnels*. Each funnel has two sides, with one of the sides always resting with the CIO. From this vantage point, the CIO facilitates communication between techies and executives in one of the funnels, between users and providers in another of the funnels, and between those inside the company and those outside the company in the third funnel. This illustrates the complexity of the communications web that the CIO must weave together with multiple, disparate constituencies to ensure success.

Figure 8.1 illustrates the complex set of triaxial communications required of a CIO. To be completely successful, CIO communications need to include all three components. In today's world, CIOs must not only master this complex, integrated web of communications, but also be comfortable being the nucleus of it.

To become competent at such communications, the CIO must understand that the nature and type of communications between and among the groups are very different. As a result, the CIO must be able to alter the content delivery medium and his or her communication style to suit each constituency.

To some extent, the CIO serves as the formal IT "Rosetta Stone" among all the different parties. That is not to say that other informal and formal communications do not occur directly between and among the parties. These occur on a regular basis. The CIO, however, sets the tone and drives the main IT messages to multiple, disparate groups.

THE POWER OF COMMUNICATIONS

In addition to being translators of information, CIOs must be considered by IT staff and executive leadership as part of their respective teams. They must be able to *relate* to and have empathy for each of their various constituencies: IT staff, leadership, users, and even outside vendors. A marketing and

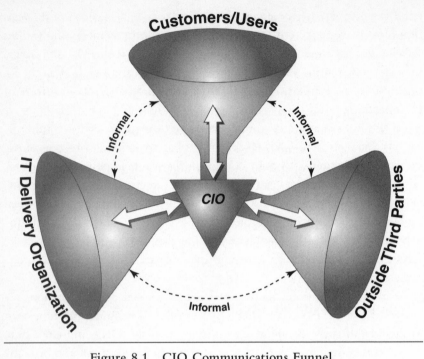

Figure 8.1   CIO Communications Funnel.

communications professional can help CIOs not only to craft their messages in terms that are meaningful to each constituency, but also to understand how every one of their actions and behaviors communicates to the various constituencies as powerfully as their words. Setting up and using mechanisms for open and honest communications allow CIOs to establish themselves as role models for others in the IT organization.

FROM CAPTIVE TO WILLING USER

Because everyone in a company uses IT, everyone is, in a sense, a captive of the IT organization. However, the goals of IT communications are to make users want to utilize IT services and to persuade them that the IT organization is a provider of high-quality, high-performance services that have significant value.

To accomplish these objectives and create willing, rather than captive, IT users, IT leaders, with the help of communications professionals, need to take the time and effort required to craft messages that place IT activities and efforts in the proper context. Then they need to instill in every member of the IT organization the notion that carrying these messages in a consistent fashion to various constituencies within and outside the company is important and is a part of every person's job.

Too many CIOs and other IT professionals are comfortable operating IT as a "black box" operation and communicate their activities on a need-to-know basis. However, if CIOs are to be invited to sit at the executive table, they must peel back the curtain and reveal how IT operates and articulate messages that help explain these operations and how they benefit the company. Transparency and open, candid communications are two ways to achieve that goal.

COMMUNICATING LIKE BUSINESS LEADERS

To manage IT as a business, CIOs must learn how to communicate like business leaders. This means properly balancing honesty and integrity with a small dose of *spin control.* Unfortunately, politics affect all organizations to some degree. Political leaders and constituencies, including the CIO and those who work in the broader IT organization, need to define how others in the company perceive them and their organizations. If they do not, others will do it for them.

At one organization with which I worked, the CIO and IT staff were, from a technical perspective, among the best I have ever seen. Despite their skills, others in the company treated them as doormats and regularly subjected them to vicious tongue-lashings. Any time an IT-related problem cropped up, these highly qualified IT professionals became the scapegoats and were put on the defensive. They were disheartened and demoralized because they knew they were doing a good job. But the CIO and the entire IT organization did not know how to get that message across effectively to the various constituencies.

The marketing/communications group persuaded the CIO to hold monthly briefing sessions with each business unit. He began to issue a marketing-quality quarterly report on IT performance, services, and projects.

Within six months, the IT organization's image improved significantly within the company, and people within the IT organization began to believe they were real contributors to the company's success.

THREE WAYS TO GET THE MESSAGE ACROSS

A CIO should engage an IT organization communications professional to assist in crafting appropriate messages tailored to specific circumstances, audiences, and purposes. Generally, corporate communications fall under one of three categories: marketing, public relations, or general communications.

Marketing

Marketing messages are communicated through various media in ways that are attractive and appealing to specific audiences. Marketing communications are crisp and brisk. Their purpose is to get the audience to internalize and accept the message quickly. In the context of IT, marketing efforts seek to build awareness of the IT organization, of its attributes, and of the role it plays in accomplishing the company's business goals.

Traditionally, external marketing media include radio, television, web sites, print advertising, brochures, letters, signs, and billboards. Although formats can differ, the purpose is always to *push* a particular message out to a specific audience. From an internal marketing perspective and for companies that use sophisticated e-mail push systems and workflow and messaging software, marketing messages can be pushed out as part of the message flow. However, because of their tendency to produce technical solutions, many CIOs and IT organizations mistakenly focus on electronic media (primarily e-mail). In almost all cases, a more appropriate combination of media is more effective.

Pull marketing is a companion to push marketing. With pull marketing, message recipients who are intrigued by a pushed message actively pull more information about a product, service, or program. Not every member of a target audience needs to connect with every aspect of a marketing effort. With pull marketing, all recipients are exposed to the basic message and allowed to pull additional information to satisfy their desire to know more.

IT organizations can use marketing to build awareness of the services they provide, current performance levels, and projects in progress. They can also use marketing to prepare various constituencies for changes to those services.

Public Relations

The field of public relations (PR) seeks to use free media to increase awareness of an organization and the esteem in which it is held. Traditional media for external public relations include press releases or announcements, press conferences, sponsorship of events or conferences, and presentations by individuals from within the organization to audiences for whom a particular message is important.

Public relations is usually defined as communications between a company and its various external constituencies. However, PR can be equally important for an organization within a company as well.

Consider a company's IT organization. When communicating to an internal audience, the CIO and all of the company's IT professionals must portray their activities as being "under control" from a performance, economic, organizational, and management perspective. To facilitate this, the IT team should undertake to perform a regular set of established formal internal IT PR related to 24/7 services and special projects.

For example, the simple act of explaining how the CIO regularly delivers even mundane services such as help desk usage statistics can provide a PR message. Providing these statistics to the business units as a detailed list in a spreadsheet sends a message: "This is a techie organization." However, adding a little narrative spin, including some trend analysis and a few well-focused, clear, color graphics, conveys a different message: "The IT group is able to measure things in a clear and concise, business-focused manner." If the statistical information and narrative is delivered in a formal briefing session rather than by e-mail, the message is taken up to yet another level, and the CIO is seen as one of the company's leaders. Because of its ability to shape perceptions, internal IT PR is an essential component of any business, particularly in today's complex, integrated, and wired environment.

Public relations can also be used to mitigate possible negative impacts of problems. This function is often referred to as *crisis PR*. Like any other business unit, IT organizations are not immune to crisis. In fact, in today's world, because IT touches just about everyone in the company, the manner in which IT crises are handled can make or break the CIO, the entire IT organization, and possibly even the company itself.

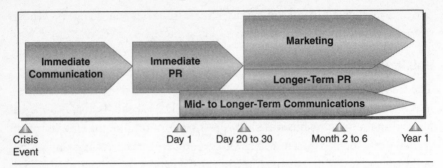

Figure 8.2 CIO Crisis Communications Overview.

Any combination of possible events can create a potential IT crisis that warrants the use of crisis PR. These events include, for example, a merger or acquisition integration mishap, a catastrophic failure of a mission-critical application, a network or critical infrastructure failure, a significant security breach or unchecked virus attack, or a physical disaster. Figure 8.2 illustrates the sequence and mix of different communications, PR, and marketing components associated with a CIO/IT crisis situation.

CASE STUDY 8.2

Public Relations to the Rescue

One of the primary central cluster locations in the office network of a large, IT-dependent maintenance services company experienced a catastrophic fire. Thankfully, the fire occurred at night and none of the more than 800 employees who worked at the site was injured or killed.

The location housed critical servers and telecommunications equipment, and, on a regular basis, local customers interacted electronically with these servers to obtain critical information. As soon as the site IT manager was paged and notified about the fire, he immediately initiated the fully tested disaster recovery plan.

Both the technical and human relations portions of the plan were executed flawlessly. Because redundancy had been designed into the applications, network, and infrastructure, including a physical backup site for employees, everything was returned to operational status within 36 hours.

However, because of the severe nature of the damage and the outage that occurred, the disaster recovery plan included a crisis PR component. Customers, as well as employees, needed to be reassured that the company's IT organization had everything under control.

Customers could use competitors to obtain the same services the company provided, and nobody in the IT organization wanted to be the cause of the company's losing business. It was critical that the IT organization help to eliminate the panic that was spreading among employees throughout the company.

The company's crisis PR strategy included direct, personal phone calls by the CIO and IT leadership team members to all key external customers and key employee group leaders (via cell phone because the office phones had been knocked out by the fire). In addition, the CIO worked with business-unit management to craft and deliver key messages to the various media, reassuring everyone that although a disaster had occurred, the situation was now stable and in recovery mode.

Finally, things settled down. Because the recovery effort had been so successful, the CIO and others in the company began to speak publicly and to write articles about how they had handled the situation. In doing so, they turned a potentially disastrous situation into an operational and technical success and a bonanza of positive PR that enhanced the company's image considerably in the eyes of customers, the marketplace as a whole, and employees.

General Communications

Beyond marketing and public relations, other communications in which the CIO or other members of the IT organization engage include:

- Regularly issued (quarterly, semiannual, annual) operating reports
- Formal organizational leadership meetings and conferences
- Open forums, which can range from brown-bag lunches to e-mail bulletin boards.

One of the most effective communication tools I have ever encountered involved a CIO's regularly scheduled personal visits to local office locations. Often linking the visits with a planning meeting, the CIO would engage in informal discussions with the IT organization's key customers/users and with business-unit management.

In addition, the CIO took the opportunity to meet with local IT staff members to talk about the organization's overall strategy and to solicit their views and concerns. These were highly successful sessions because everyone involved derived something positive from them. They created a win-win environment.

As soon as the CIO would leave a location, staff would be on the phone or writing e-mail trying to set up a date for the next visit. The direct, personal approach the CIO used to clearly communicate—verbally, in writing, and through his actions—created substantial trust and credibility among users, business-units leaders, and IT staff alike.

FRAMING THE IT ORGANIZATION MESSAGE

Whether the message is delivered in a marketing, public relations, or general communications format, it must be clear, consistent, and meaningful to the intended audience. To create the proper messages from the IT organization to its various constituencies, the CIO and others in IT leadership must develop an understanding of each constituency's perception of value and of how the IT organization provides that value.

Communications should be linked, both explicitly and implicitly, to the company's business strategy, not merely to the IT strategy. IT's role in supporting and enabling that strategy should be woven into the IT organization's message. Because quality, cost, and service delivery are the IT organization's key deliverables, messages should focus on how IT is progressing on improving these areas.

Success relating to communications efforts should be defined before those efforts are begun. The IT leadership should have a clear goal for its communications program and a vision of how it wants various audiences and constituencies to respond to its messages. To that end, leadership should address the following questions:

- What actions does the IT organization want the particular constituency to take?

- What change does the IT organization want to promote concerning the perception of IT value (i.e., instilling in users an understanding of the tradeoff between cost and service level)?
- What message does the IT organization want a particular audience (e.g., business-unit leaders) to convey to another audience (e.g., users within business units)?
- What short- and long-term impact or results does the IT organization anticipate?
- What are the IT organization's contingency plans in case the communication efforts are not as effective or successful as IT leadership would like them to be?

CASE STUDY 8.3

The Day One Marketing Campaign

Within a few years of assuming his position, the CIO of a large, global-construction management services company had pushed and prodded both the IT organization and the company into making major changes. He had used the skills and business sense he had honed as an operating executive to begin managing the IT organization as if it were a business.

By engaging in open and honest dialogue with other key executives about the proper role of IT as an enabler of meeting the company's business goals and objectives, he had become an accepted part of the corporate leadership team. He and the IT organization had made headway in improving their own processes and in helping users to recognize that IT services are not free and that tradeoffs exist concerning what a company is willing to spend on IT and the level of service users can expect.

Over several years, the company had come to understand its total IT spend; had identified the IT assets it possessed; had consolidated IT operations; and had standardized PCs, server platforms, and application software suites. The IT organization had been stabilized to a point where the CIO and his top IT managers could begin to think about longer term and more rational planning.

When all of this had been accomplished, the company's leadership decided to acquire another company in the same business and of relatively the same size. Although the executives of both companies tried hard to ensure that neither company dominated the transaction, it was clear that the CIO's company was much further along in managing IT as a business. For this reason, it was clear that the CIO would fill the same role in the newly formed company.

Essentially, he would again have to take the lead in creating a vision for an IT organization that involved understanding the IT spend and then consolidating, rationalizing, standardizing, and upgrading hardware, software, processes, and skills. He organized a set of IT integration-planning teams and set to work on a 90-day crash effort to ensure that on Day One of the newly formed company's existence, four elements would be in place:

1. Individuals throughout the company would be able to continue to access critical manufacturing, supply chain, marketing and sales, finance, and HR systems and data.
2. They would be able to communicate with one another by e-mail and share documents created in different formats.
3. Over 50,000 people in offices in more than 45 countries would be able to access technical help anywhere at any time.
4. In the IT organization, there would be no "us" and "them" but only a single team working to provide world-class service to users throughout the newly formed company to help enable the company to reach its business goals and objectives.

Communicating effectively across such a large organization was a daunting task. A newly established group of nearly 500 IT staff members spread around the world would have to be educated, primed, and inculcated with a vision of providing high-performance and quality work under extreme time pressure.

Under the CIO's direction, teams from the two different companies began sorting out how they would work together well in advance of Day One. A multifaceted approach was required to address the marketing and communications needs of users and other constituencies and, within the IT organization, to deal with change management and team-building issues related to an all-encompassing IT integration. The sheer volume and variety of required communications—aimed at different constituencies, for different purposes, and in different formats—were astounding.

Setting expectations was the key theme that unified all communications. Although the CIO had a marketing and communications professional as a member of his key IT leadership team, that individual was not going to be able to handle all the work that had to get done in the compressed time frame before Day One. The CIO, therefore, engaged an outside communications-consulting firm that also had experience in the HR and behavioral issues related to change management.

A communications task force led by the IT communications leader was established and charged with the responsibility of preparing an overall Day One marketing and communications campaign and then of developing and streaming the appropriate communications to the right people at the right time.

Because the possibility of information overload and boredom was a problem, the communications effort was structured as a marketing campaign. Staff members from the two companies were being bombarded with detailed communications from all parts of the enterprise. Each separate communication from the IT organization was kept short and was tightly focused on actions required at that time. Because of the tendency of employees to procrastinate when asked to take actions of an IT nature (e.g., backing up data, deleting or archiving e-mail, or upgrading a piece of application software), a series of properly timed and increasingly intense communications were sent out to compel individuals to take action.

The communications task force focused a great deal of attention on a critical marketing piece, a "Day One Technology Success Guide." The CIO suggested that the guide be available in hard copy because some people might not be able to access it online or download it to their hard drives. The guide answered users' Day One questions about getting IT support and assistance, using the e-mail system and database capabilities, accessing the Internet, using telephones and voice mail, handling specific software conversion issues, and obtaining training and instruction. The guide also listed all key company resources.

The guide was deployed electronically and was also issued as a set of laminated cards of varying sizes. These cards were placed in a narrow folder so that either the entire folder or individual cards would fit in the inner pocket of a suit coat or in the outside pocket of a soft briefcase or backpack.

Internal communications reported on a series of regional IT leadership meetings that focused on vision, strategy, and integration plans and on team building and relationship development. In addition, key business-unit executives from each of the regions of the world where the company operated were invited to participate in meetings with regional IT leadership to begin strengthening those relationships.

In addition to communicating within the IT organization and executing an IT marketing effort targeted to users, IT leaders also needed to meet and communicate with outside business partners and vendors to gain a better understanding of the roles they would be asked to play before, during, and after Day One and with the newly formed company. Key global, national, and local vendors of hardware, software, and services were invited to participate in some segments of the IT regional meetings.

Finally, before Day One, the CIO addressed some HR/behavioral issues that were counterproductive to the integration effort. Unfortunately, he had been unsuccessful at eliminating all the stonewalling, power struggles, and inappropriate behavior that had sprung up among those angry with or fearful of the changes necessary within the IT organization. The CIO engaged some professional behaviorists to work personally with some of the more difficult individuals in an attempt to allay their fears, reduce their anger, and help them accommodate to change. The goal was not to punish them; many were highly skilled individuals who could contribute greatly to the effort. Rather, the goal was to provide the extra attention some people needed so that they could be brought on board with any change.

The net result of all of these communications and interpersonal efforts was to focus attention within the IT organization, executive leadership group, business units, and outside business partners and among users throughout the organization on important changes that were going to occur in the IT operations as part of the Day One integration efforts. In the IT organization, the focus was on creating an environment that encouraged IT staff members and others to join the team, to take responsibility for delivering specific, measurable results, and to work at a high-performance level. In addition, one of the primary reasons for concentrating so much effort on communications was to ensure that reasonable and realistic expectations were set concerning what IT could and could not do and what it would and would not deliver on Day One.

WHAT THE CEO CAN DO TO ENSURE THAT COMMUNICATIONS ARE INTEGRAL TO THE CIO'S PERFORMANCE AND SUCCESS

Often, effective marketing, public relations, and communications skills are not considered high priorities for CIOs. However, like any other major business unit in a company, the IT organization must effectively communicate on a regular basis with all of its constituents and customers.

CEOs can take five concrete steps to ensure that communications are integral to the CIO's overall performance and success:

1. Ensure that the CIO uses professional marketing and communications assistance on a regular basis; assign a marketing/communications professional to work directly with the CIO.
2. Require that the CIO communicate on a regular basis to leadership and to the management team in a format and style that best facilitates understanding the messages the CIO is trying to get across.
3. Make sure that the CIO and members of the IT organization understand that an important part of their performance assessment will focus on how well they communicate with one another and with the various constituencies of the IT organization.
4. Ensure that the CIO has performance information on marketing/communications as one of the key items on his or her IT management/value measurement dashboard.
5. Encourage business unit and corporate management to create town hall-type events that include the CIO and members of the IT organization. Such events encourage open and honest communication and foster discussion of issues about performance, plans, and long-term strategies.

CHAPTER 9

Information Technology Improvement Never Ends

CASE STUDY 9.1

They Thought Their Work Was Done

The CIO of a large mining and chemicals company had been hard at work for three years restructuring the company's global IT organization to ensure that it was aligned with the business. Significant progress had been made, and the CIO considered the effort to be in the home stretch. After years of constant change, everyone in the IT organization was looking forward to a period of stability.

In a sense, the IT staff was beginning to feel as if they had reached the end of their journey and had created a "new IT" organization. However, just as they were beginning to celebrate, the CEO made a stunning announcement: He had agreed to a merger with another mining company that was similar in size and scope of business. The new company would have approximately 55,000 people located in 42 countries.

Serving as a backdrop to the integration that would have to be accomplished were a host of very complex cultural and political issues that went beyond business units, geography, and functional boundaries. In addition to regulatory issues, these would not be settled until fairly late in the process, leaving a minimum amount of time for addressing critical IT integration and operational matters.

Despite the many issues that could not be immediately settled, teams from each company were established to perform the typical due diligence activities related to financial, legal, and customer service matters. Team members were given three weeks to complete their work. Because the executive teams recognized up front that IT would be a key enabler for the merger, a separate IT due diligence team was established.

The two IT organizations were very different. One company had spent the previous three years restructuring its entire approach to global IT—including upgrading the entire IT infrastructure, establishing a cohesive and unified global IT organization, making the CIO an integral part of the executive management team, and creating tight linkages among local, regional, and business-unit operating leaders. The other company, however, had just begun to globalize its IT organization and operations. At this company, IT was run on a local level. No single authority existed for operational IT matters, resource/skill management, or IT budgeting. Whereas one company had completely standardized its entire IT infrastructure, including PC hardware, software, and services, the other company was running myriad hardware platforms and software applications and providing service locally.

Each team designated people to participate in the IT due diligence effort. One company supplied the global CIO and his major direct reports. These individuals had operational, financial, and HR responsibilities for global IT activities. The other company supplied its European IT leader, its U.S. IT technical leader, and two other technical managers. Given the disparity in the makeup of the teams, some disagreement understandably existed about the areas to be included in the due diligence process. One company wanted to look only at technical matters while the other wanted to include IT management issues as well. Three meetings were required before team members could agree on the importance of IT management issues.

Other individuals from each company joined the primary IT due diligence teams to collect and analyze data that was being made available. At the completion of the IT due diligence process, the team members jointly prepared a formal report that included a gap analysis comparing the relative position of each company with respect to each of the comparison categories.

At the end of the due diligence effort, the members of the new executive team of the soon-to-be-merged company named as CIO the individual from the company with the more advanced IT organization. Although he was excited, he was not rattled by this choice because he felt confident that he had already built a high-performance, high-quality, and very agile global IT organization that would be able to deal quickly with enormous change.

The new CIO set about the task of merging and integrating two highly disparate global IT organizations. His focus was on ensuring that IT could do its part to enable a smooth transition. It would not be easy, and the organization that had thought it could cruise to the finish line would have to run another long race. However, he knew his experiences over the previous three years would stand him and his organization in good stead.

The bottom line in this case study is that in a modern IT organization, the only constant is change. Nobody can predict the exact nature of the change at any point in time or the impact of major business changes on IT. Therefore, the most important task for the CIO and the IT organization is to establish a solid but adaptable foundation that will enable the organization to absorb and deal effectively with continuous change.

When flexibility, agility, and high performance are institutionalized, the CIO and the entire IT organization can rapidly adjust to new business conditions, including major strategic changes such as large mergers, acquisitions, or divestitures.

IT organizations that believe their work is finished when they complete a series of discrete projects are captives of a rigidity that will disable their ability to keep up with real changes occurring in the business. CIOs and IT organizations that are positioned to embrace change can easily absorb a continuous flow of new requirements over long periods of time and be flexible and agile enough to become a company's true enablers.

CASE STUDY 9.2

How IT Makes Change Possible

A large beauty products company wished to acquire certain brands that resided in a division of a European competitor. Purchase of the division was deemed anticompetitive by regulators in Europe and North America. As a solution, it was proposed that the acquiring company create a joint venture with a third company to purchase the division and then disaggregate it, assigning some brands to the original acquirer and others to the joint venture partner.

Although regulators viewed this solution more favorably, they mandated that confidentiality of competitive data be protected throughout the two-stage transaction. This meant that the joint venture needed to be up and running as of the closing date of the transaction and that, for information and reporting purposes, the target division needed to be split apart on closing.

An alternative structure was created. Until the target's operations could be wound down in an orderly manner, the joint venture would handle confidential information independently of either acquiring party. Given the high degree of supply chain automation at the target, developing adequate control processes and splitting the IT infrastructure were of critical importance.

In addition, for the deal to work, the processes and IT infrastructure of the target company needed to be separated in a way that would support outright sale of certain brands as well as temporary separate operation of other brands. Before the acquisition could be finalized, roles, responsibilities, and plans to support the carve-out needed to be agreed on.

To comply with the regulators' prohibition against sharing certain marketing information, the company's IT staff had to define processes and information flows within the parameters of a firewall and to specify the time frames, the roles and responsibilities, and the nature of the information to be shared at each stage of the transaction.

Despite the delicacy of the information integration issues created by the regulators' mandates, the company successfully completed the acquisition and added brands that significantly strengthened the company's market position. The integration of both the brands and of the people associated with those brands was, in the words of some business leaders who observed the transaction, "incredibly successful."

Whatever is happening in the IT organization today will not be happening tomorrow. Some constants run themselves over time—for example, the ongoing provision of IT services that are measured with static metrics. However, much of the work of the IT organization is dynamic.

Yet that does not mean that, as an organization, IT is reactive. Although employees throughout the IT organization must be able to react to changes in the company's goals and objectives and to produce business value to meet those goals and objectives, their ability to make these tactical changes is derived from a set of strategic, proactive decisions made by the IT organization's leaders, especially the CIO.

Like any business, an IT organization is sometimes compared to a shark—keep swimming or die—or to a virus—keep changing, or someone will figure out how to neutralize you. In the world of IT, the IT organization that remains static is the IT organization that will not be able to perform at consistently high levels and continue to add value to the business.

Static IT organizations cost too much and allow service levels to deteriorate and project deadlines to slip. All of these outgrowths of stasis in an IT organization have a direct impact on the company's ability to maintain its competitive advantage in an environment in which the company's ability is, increasingly, a competitive differentiator.

CREATING AN INNOVATIVE ORGANIZATION

CASE STUDY 9.3
The Power of Trust, Teamwork, and Relationships

After completing the due diligence effort, the newly appointed CIO in the merged company described earlier in this chapter was faced with the daunting task of building, in a very short time frame, a single, integrated IT team with a unified vision and mission. The CIO decided that the joint IT integration team should be kept as small as possible and should include only the most critical strategic, technical, functional, and geographic representation from each company.

The team held several preliminary integration sessions. At these sessions, team members agreed that the most efficient way to identify the real issues was to convene a three-day, in-depth IT integration planning meeting involving at least the first layer of key IT management and technical staff from each company. The objective of this meeting would be to assess the IT infrastructures in each company with a view toward establishing plans for integration. In addition, leadership felt that this meeting would provide a good forum for developing key personal relationships among all members of IT management.

At the meeting, team members conducted an in-depth assessment of the companies' current IT infrastructures. The assessment included a thorough analysis and documentation of the present operations. This exercise prepared the team, as much as possible, to proceed rapidly to support and enable the business strategy decisions that would be made as soon as the companies were merged. The IT team sought to create a sufficiently detailed fact base from which the members could assess the future business decisions that would be made by the merged company's executive management team. They could then rapidly translate those assessments into executable IT action plans that would provide the support necessary to achieve interoperability on Day One among members of what had been the two former companies.

The goal was not to preestablish, preempt, or presuppose any of those decisions. Rather, it was to identify possible alternatives and options and their relative impacts, costs, and benefits. However, the underlying objective of the meeting was to begin the process of establishing trust, teamwork, and key relationships.

Some of the key issues addressed during the IT integration meeting included defining the overall IT vision, identifying the primary integration requirements and key activities, reviewing the main challenges, assessing the potential risks, developing the overall integration strategy, determining the preliminary costs and benefits, and defining the actions required to move forward.

The meeting was very productive. It clearly demonstrated that the IT staffs of the two companies could, in fact, work seamlessly and easily together as they focused on meeting the new company's business needs. The meeting helped to initiate the critical relationships needed to execute a complex global IT combination successfully.

Too often, CIOs and members of the IT organization are comfortable only when things are totally under control, which is never the case.

Driving every aspect of IT operations to a place where the entire IT domain is static is impossible. Even if it were possible, obsolescence and high cost would rapidly follow. Because of the rapid change in technology combined with constantly changing company goals and objectives, IT leadership needs to ensure that members of the organization are adaptive and able to *innovate while things are happening.*

IT is not comparable to a fully sequential engineering system in which deliverables result from planning, designing, building, testing, reworking, retesting, and finalizing. The IT organization is more like an immune system that senses a change in the environment, harnesses the resources to respond, and builds and tests the response on the fly. Such an organization can come into being only in an atmosphere of trust, teamwork, and selflessness.

BALANCING IT RISKS

The twenty-first century CEO, business-unit leader, or CIO will have to work with teams as never before to align and balance the four key IT business risks with the company's primary business objectives. These risks are:

1. *Economic risk:* The appropriateness of the IT spend and the alignment of the IT investment portfolio with business goals.
2. *Organizational and process risk:* The appropriateness of IT management and technical skills and practices.
3. *Performance risk:* The performance of IT relative to industry peers and an individual company's size and growth plans.
4. *Crisis risk:* The degree to which IT is contributing to the protection of a company's day-to-day operations with respect to business continuity, data quality, and security.

The company's IT business risk exposure needs to be evaluated against the key underlying drivers of total IT spend, investments, resources, assets, controls, and overall business value. Figure 9.1 illustrates in more detail the key IT business risks.

DEVELOPING NEW CIOS

One of the most important tasks of a CEO and a CIO is to develop a succession plan and groom a successor. Like CEOs, CIOs are often judged by the number of other CIOs that they have helped to develop.

A CIO's job will be a lot easier if he or she develops a management team containing potential CIOs—those individuals who, at a moment's notice, are prepared to assume the role of CIO on a temporary or permanent basis. With both a trusted second-in-command and a host of talented managers on board, a CIO can travel to meet with IT employees, business-unit

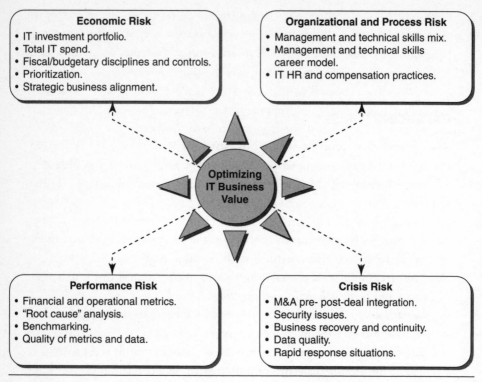

Economic Risk
- IT investment portfolio.
- Total IT spend.
- Fiscal/budgetary disciplines and controls.
- Prioritization.
- Strategic business alignment.

Organizational and Process Risk
- Management and technical skills mix.
- Management and technical skills career model.
- IT HR and compensation practices.

Optimizing IT Business Value

Performance Risk
- Financial and operational metrics.
- "Root cause" analysis.
- Benchmarking.
- Quality of metrics and data.

Crisis Risk
- M&A pre- post-deal integration.
- Security issues.
- Business recovery and continuity.
- Data quality.
- Rapid response situations.

Figure 9.1   Balancing IT Business Risks.

leaders, and users throughout the corporation and know that the IT organization will continue to function well.

These potential CIOs will not necessarily be technologists. Because the CIO role is a business leadership position, potential CIOs can come from the ranks of those embedded throughout the company whose specialty is finance, marketing, law, or human resources. The key question to ask of a potential CIO successor is: How will you cope with and manage within a state of constant change?

The best way to develop future CIOs is not necessarily to anoint individuals or a small group and then shower them with extra attention. The best way is to create an IT organization whose members adhere to common decision-making principles, know how to focus on the goals and objectives of the business and how to use the IT organization to reach those goals and objectives, and possess the skills and mind-set required to work in a state of constant change. From such an organization, future leaders will naturally rise to the top.

Most CEOs do not expect CIOs to focus on the issue of succession or on developing leadership talent. But why shouldn't they? After all, business-unit leaders are expected to play this role. If the CIO is going to change from being the manager of a support function to being the leader of an enabling business unit, he or she is going to have to manage and think like a business leader.

The CIO at one organization with which I spent some time devoted a significant amount of effort to working with and cultivating the IT management team and to encouraging them to always take on new challenges by stepping out of their existing roles. As a result, her key IT managers developed a broad range of new IT management and technical skills.

As this CIO's IT management team became more and more experienced, many members left the corporate IT group to take on CIO roles within the company's many divisions. Whereas some corporate CIOs might see this as a talent drain, this CIO felt it was a key part of her job to develop new CIOs by moving people from her IT organization into the business units so that they could take on increased responsibilities. Over time, this approach established a cadre of well-trained, independent IT executives (not clones) throughout the company who functioned extremely well together in defining business-unit and corporate goals and in making sure the business-unit and global IT organizations worked well together to help the business meet those goals.

CONTROLLING THE PROCESS OF ADDRESSING CHANGE

Nobody can control the rate or degree of change—both in technology and in the demands of a business. However, people can control the organizational dynamics of addressing change by managing and leading in a professional manner and by focusing rigorously on priorities, people, and performance.

As illustrated in Figure 9.2, effectively managing priorities, people, and performance is key to managing the components of the IT improvement process. These components include:

- Establishing an IT capability baseline
- Benchmarking the IT organization's capabilities

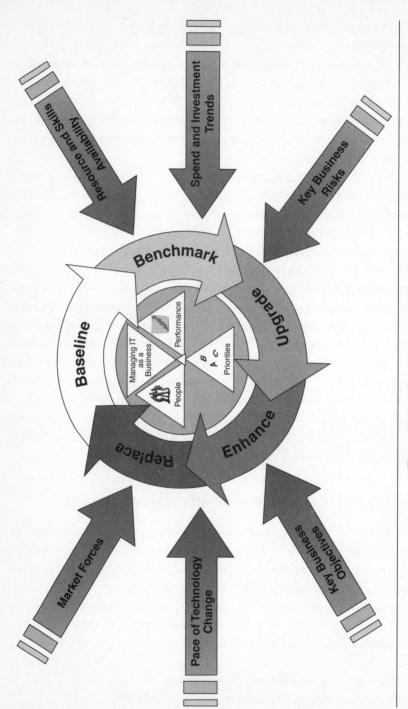

Figure 9.2 IT Improvement Cycle.

234

- Upgrading those capabilities, as appropriate
- Enhancing those capabilities by taking them to a new level
- Replacing outdated and ineffective capabilities with new, more effective ones.

The IT organization must continuously iterate this IT improvement cycle while dealing with and absorbing multiple forces of change—changes in market forces, key business objectives, key business risks, the pace of technology, IT spend and investment trends, and availability of IT resources and skills.

Effective CEOs, business-unit leaders, and CIOs working together in twenty-first century companies can master and harness the people, priority, and performance drivers of the entire IT organization. This book has attempted to provide some practical guidance on how to work together and on how to understand one another's roles in the totality of the effort. Although accomplishing this will not be a cakewalk, those corporate leaders who understand and act on these messages will be at the forefront of the movement to *manage IT as a business*. They will also be laying a strong foundation for the future success of their IT organization and their business.

THE CEO'S ROLE IN SETTING AN IT AGENDA FOR THE TWENTY-FIRST CENTURY

Learning how to manage IT as a business cannot be accomplished in a two-day executive education course. It is learned primarily through apprenticeship, as individuals work together over time in teams with people who do it well, who understand the positive implications of doing it well, and who are willing to act as role models for others.

Nevertheless, to ensure that they have in place the *right stuff* from which they can project an effective IT agenda for the twenty-first century, CEOs need to answer five key questions:

1. Can I trust my CIO to run a major operating business unit in my company?
2. If not, what steps can I take to ensure that he or she could become the CEO of one of my major business units?

3. What do I personally do on a daily basis to make sure that my CIO has or is developing the skills he or she needs to succeed and that he or she will be welcomed as an equal member at the executive table?

4. How effective am I at really understanding (and have I taken the time to truly understand) how IT can be used to enable and drive certain aspects of my business?

5. If today, IT as we currently know it were to disappear from my company, what would be the impact of that disappearance?

Index